C. F. ANDREWS

Friends of India Series II
Series Editor: Mushirul Hasan

C. F. ANDREWS FRIEND OF INDIA

Nicol Macnicol, D.LITT., D.D.

NIYOGI BOOKS

Published by

NIYOGI BOOKS

D-78, Okhla Industrial Area, Phase-I
New Delhi-110 020, India
Tel: 91-11-26816301, 49327000
Fax: 91-11-26810483, 26813830
email: niyogibooks@gmail.com
www.niyogibooksindia.com

ISBN: 978-93-81523-77-3
Year of Publication: 2013

Printed at: Niyogi Offset Pvt. Ltd., New Delhi, India

Contents

'Christ's Faithful Apostle': C.F. Andrews

He came to Delhi, his 'first love', in April 1904 to promote the Cambridge Brotherhood. He guided St Stephen's College, an 'Alexandria on the Banks of the Jamuna' in the years from 1904 to 1913. He was the 33-year-old Charles Freer Andrews.

What does he tell us? According to Hugh Tinker, 'Charlie Andrews remained the unique individual who had stepped out of his position as a foreigner, a stranger to India, into the lives and hearts of Indians in order to show that nationality and race were infinitely less important than brotherhood and love.' India's Deenabandhu, 'friend of the poor' lived in the joys and sorrows of Indians, their triumphs and misfortunes.

Of all the British friends in India, in the early twentieth century, Andrews understood Indian aspirations better than most. The vessel of his life found anchorage in Santiniketan, 'the Abode of Peace'. *Gitanjali* bound him up with India's life, while Rabindranath Tagore made him give up his arduous wanderings to be with him. It brought him fulfillment during years of alternating action and contemplation.

He became Gandhi's *bhakt* as well: their hearts met from the first moment they saw each other, and they remained united by the strongest ties of love. Andrews found that Truth, loving kindness, and inner purity pervade all of Gandhi's writings and actions. He was therefore an inspiration that awakened all that was best in Andrews and gave him a high courage, enkindled and enlightened by his own. He disagreed with Gandhi's recruitment campaign for the war, non-cooperation, and the excessive reliance on fasts, and yet a harmony of spirit brought the two closer to each other.

Theirs was a friendship of equals; they were 'Mohan' and 'Charlie' to each other. All the circumstances of their situation seemed to draw them together; they were like two long-lost friends who go hand in hand, pressing closely to each other through the passage of life. Once, Gandhi implored Tagore 'to lend me Mr. Andrews now and then. His guidance at times is most precious to me.' He filled the pages of *Young India* with thankful praise of him.

Charlie, in turn, died with the satisfaction of having had many friends. He remarked at his deathbed: 'God has given me in life the greatest of all gifts—namely, the gift of loving friends. At this moment when I am laying my life in His hands I would like to acknowledge again, what I have acknowledged in my books; this supreme gift of friendship.'

Biographies of Andrews are not in short supply. Hugh Tinker wrote *The Ordeal of Love: C.F. Andrews and India* (1979), a book of considerable merit; equally, the revised edition of Daniel O'Connor's *A Clear Star: C.F. Andrews and India, 1904-1914* (2005) is a delightful read. We are pleased to reprint a highly readable biography by an author who belonged to Andrews' Christian tradition, and appreciated, probably for this reason, the role and contribution of a wise, erudite, and morally upright individual.

When I reprinted *Zaka Ullah of Delhi* by Andrews and *Inside India* by Halide Edib with the Oxford University Press, I noticed a great deal of interest in them. The reader's response gave me the idea of reprinting certain classical works that may open up new areas of research.

This reprint is the first in the series 'Friends of India'. We invite friends and colleagues to suggest books and monographs that can be reprinted in this series.

Mushirul Hasan

MODERN CHRISTIAN REVOLUTIONARIES SERIES

General Editor:

DONALD ATTWATER

C. F. ANDREWS: FRIEND OF INDIA

He who praises a man ought to follow him, and if he be not ready to follow him he ought not to praise him.—*St. John Chrysostom.*

MODERN CHRISTIAN REVOLUTIONARIES

C. F. ANDREWS: FRIEND OF INDIA

By

NICOL MACNICOL, D.LITT., D.D.

His love for Indians was a part of that love of all mankind which he accepted as the law of Christ.—*Rabindranath Tagore.*

JAMES CLARKE & CO., LTD.
5 WARDROBE PLACE, CARTER LANE, LONDON, E.C.4

TO

THE MEMORY OF

WILLIAM PATON

Printed in Great Britain by
The Camelot Press Ltd., London and Southampton

PREFACE

This little book was to have been written by Dr William Paton, whose knowledge of India and friendship with C. F. Andrews eminently fitted him for the task. He had collected his material and was about to begin upon it when, in August of last year, his sudden death prevented this among the many enterprises to which the need of the time had called him. It was in these circumstances that I was asked to take his place. I felt constrained to do so because of my admiration and affection for him, as well as because of the interest that I shared with him in India and the service rendered to India by C. F. Andrews.

This is not intended to be a biography of Andrews. The task of preparing that will be undertaken as soon as circumstances permit, and it is the hope of Miss Agatha Harrison (the Literary Executor of C. F. Andrews) that it will be the joint work of a British and an Indian author. What this book seeks to provide is a brief survey and estimate of Andrews's life and work. Miss Harrison has helped me by supplying me with valuable material from what she herself has collected. I have also received permission from Messrs Hodder and Stoughton and Messrs Allen and Unwin to quote largely from books by Andrews published by them, especially his *What I Owe to Christ*, published by the former, and *Mahatma Gandhi's Ideas*, published by the latter. To these publishers I desire to make grateful acknowledgment. I am also much indebted to Miss Harrison and to Mr Henry Polak for reading my manuscript and making suggestions for its improvement, and to Mr. Donald Attwater, general editor of this series, for much help in preparing the manuscript for press.

It is right that mention should be made here, as evidence of the fruitfulness of Andrews's life, that since his death his friends in India, Hindu, Muslim, Christian, are planning a memorial of him in the form of "a hall of Christian culture," "for the study of the teaching and character of Christ."

N. M.

July, 1944.

BOOKS BY C. F. ANDREWS

The Relation of Christianity to the Conflict between Capital and Labour. (Burney Prize Essay, 1894.) Methuen, 1896.

North India. (Handbooks of English Church Expansion). A. Mowbray, 1908.

The Renaissance in India. The United Council for Missionary Study, 1912.

Christ and Labour. Student Christian Movement Press, 1923.

Letters to a Friend. By Rabindranath Tagore. Edited by C. F. Andrews. Allen & Unwin, 1928.

Zaka Ullah of Delhi. Heffer and Sons, Cambridge. 1929.

Mahatma Gandhi: His own Story. Edited by C. F. Andrews. Allen & Unwin, 1930.

India and the Simon Report. Allen & Unwin, 1930.

Mahatma Gandhi's Ideas. Allen & Unwin, 1931.

Mahatma Gandhi at Work: His own Story Continued. Edited by C. F. Andrews. Allen & Unwin, 1931.

What I Owe to Christ. Hodder & Stoughton, 1932.

Christ in the Silence. Hodder & Stoughton, 1933.

Sadhu Sunder Singh: A Personal Memoir. Hodder & Stoughton, 1934.

India and Britain: a Moral Challenge. S.C.M. Press, 1935.

The Indian Earthquake. Allen & Unwin, 1935.

John White of Mashonaland. Hodder & Stoughton, 1935.

India and the Pacific. Allen & Unwin, 1937.

Christ and Prayer. Hodder & Stoughton, 1937.

Christ and Human Need. Hodder & Stoughton, 1937.

The True India: a Plea for Understanding. Allen & Unwin, 1939.

The Rise and Growth of the Congress in India. With Girija Mookerjee. Allen & Unwin, 1939.

The Good Shepherd. Hodder & Stoughton, 1940.

The Sermon on the Mount. Allen & Unwin, 1942.

CONTENTS

1

Charles Freer Andrews

CHARLES FREER ANDREWS was born at Carlisle on February 12, 1871, the fourth child in a family of fourteen. The stock from which he came on his father's side belonged mainly to East Anglia. He himself looked back to them as being "religious leaders and preachers of the strict Puritan faith." Of his father he says, "Following the dictates of conscience as a minister of religion, he spent himself night and day during the whole of a long lifetime in a crowded Midland town, where there was no comeliness of nature, no beauty of the countryside, no leisure for mystical contemplation" (*What I Owe to Christ*, p. 32).

The town described in such unflattering terms was Birmingham and there his early life after the age of six was spent. His father was a minister of the Catholic Apostolic Church, a religious body that derives from the remarkable personality of Edward Irving, a prophetic figure who for a few years until his early death in 1834 obtained by his eloquence a great position, numbering among his admirers such men as Canning and Carlyle and Coleridge. Andrews came to recognize long afterwards that one thing at least that the Catholic Apostolic Church bore witness to was urgently required by the world—what he describes as "a renewal of those excellent gifts of the Holy Spirit which the Apostolic age had received in fullest measure." In spite of elements in his parents' church that repelled him, he agreed with it in his desire for a return to "first-century Christianity" (*op. cit.*, p. 209).

But deep as was Andrews's reverence for the devout lives that his parents lived and for their loyalty to the teachings of their church he presently found it impossible to remain along with them within its fellowship. At a later period in his spiritual development, however, he recognized the debt he owed to them and perhaps even to the humble congregation among whom with his parents he worshipped in those early and formative years. He remained in all his wanderings in close relation with them, realizing that what they were and what they, and especially his mother, did for him "left a permanent mark such as nothing could obliterate or remove." He was, however, to pass through a spiritual crisis which was, no doubt, closely related to the ministries of a deeply Christian home and which he recognized as his conversion.

This "deep inner change" which "changed the very scenery of daily existence" came to him when at the age of nineteen he was about to leave school and enter the University of Cambridge (*op. cit.*, Cap. V). He tells us how "without warning, the strong conviction of sin and of impurity came upon me with overpowering strength . . . and I knew myself as I really was." It might have been the experience of St. Paul or St. Augustine or anyone in any age who is confronted by God and cries, "O wretched man that I am, who shall deliver me?" Then followed with him as with them, when the night had passed and the day dawned, "a new and wonderful sense of peace and forgiveness stealing into my life at its very centre and bringing infinite relief." It is a story often told and never stale or common, the rebirth of a soul. It is necessary that we should set forth as central to the whole significance of Charles Andrews's life this event and what it meant to him. To omit it would be to omit the key to all he did and was. Again and again he bears witness through all the labours of his life to its centrality and to the power of a new life that it brought to him and that was constantly renewed at its source. Forty years later, describing in his spiritual autobiography what happened to him on that night of revelation, he writes, "Christ has been the living Christ to me ever since. . . . I have known the secret of his presence here and now as a daily reality. . . . It was the love of Christ within my heart which now began to constrain my life and mould my whole character. This is, essentially, what I owe to Christ" (*op. cit.*, pp. 95, 103).

These passages from his own account of what happened to him on that fateful night and morning can never be left out of account in any estimate of what C. F. Andrews did in the service of mankind or of what he was in his own inner being. "*Ecce Deus,*" he could say, "*fortior me qui veniens dominabitur mihi.*" The source of the power over him of this experience has been sufficiently indicated, but it may further guide us in our understanding of how the experience entered into and shaped him if we note two comments with which he himself concludes the chapter in which he unveils his own secret. "There was no need for me," he writes, "to formulate this in a creed. It was a spiritual consciousness that had come to me, not an intellectual definition; and whenever I have gone aside from that spiritual basis in order to define in metaphysical terms what I believe, it has seemed to me to bring weakness instead of strength, uncertainty instead of truth." These words make clear to us his characteristic attitude to this revelation that had come to him and that was to come again and again.

From this revelation there followed as its consequence then and always the realized and accepted duty of service, the service of love. "Almost the next day," he goes on, "I began to put this new found joy into practice. Near the church wherein I had worshipped . . . there was a slum quarter where drunkenness and vice were forced upon the poor by their very poverty itself. Never before had I even dreamt of visiting these homes or seeing these poor people. But now they became very dear to me for Christ's sake. . . . In this way the weeks and months went by, and the vision of Christ remained with me all the while" (*op. cit.*, pp. 103–4).

§

He had won a scholarship at Pembroke College, Cambridge, and in October, 1890, his college life began. It becomes evident from this time on—and increasingly as the years pass—that it was personal relationships of admiration and affection and the ties that they created that meant most to him in his life. From such relationships in large measure he derived his strength, and to them, no doubt, he owed some of his limitations. In the relationship into which he came with his divine Lord, as he himself has described it to us—a relationship of personal devotion—we find the archetype of his life. He lived by the giving and receiving of affection and his spirit was always open to this traffic. It was indeed, as we have just heard him declare, "a spiritual consciousness, not an intellectual definition," that came to him at his conversion.

Cambridge opened wide to him doors of friendship that enriched this new experience and guided and shaped his course. There he had, he tells us, "the unique good fortune" at the very beginning of his university career to have as his college tutor, Charles Hermann Prior. To him Andrews owed much during the years when "the old naïve beliefs of his childhood" were passing away and his life being reoriented. Chief among the trials that he had to face was the breach with his parents when he found it necessary to abandon elements in the faith which he had taken over from them and to shape a new course for himself. At this crisis in particular he was greatly assisted by another friendship that was granted to him, that of Basil Westcott, the youngest son of that bishop of Durham who holds so high a place among Johannine scholars. Basil Westcott was, he tells us, "the dearest companion I had in the world among those of my own age at college." The Westcott family became from this time on one of the most potent influences of his whole life.

By the time that Andrews had finished his studies in Cambridge he had made up his mind to be ordained to the ministry of the Church of England. It was also clear to him that his sphere of work, wherever it was, must be among the poor. His tutor, realizing that he was "too much of a dreamer," arranged that he should go as a lay worker to one of the most poverty-stricken districts of the Durham diocese, Monkwearmouth. There he would have to face "the concrete realities of practical life." His apprenticeship for the life of service of the poor that awaited him began here accordingly in 1895 and was continued in the Pembroke College Mission, Walworth, where he was among "the poorest and most neglected of London's poor" (*op. cit.*, pp. 123, 136).

When this period of training was completed he was ordained to the Anglican ministry, though he tells us that he had many doubts and hesitations to overcome concerning some of the "articles of religion" which he was required to sign and some of the duties that he would have, as a clergyman of the Church of England, to discharge. The recitation of the "cursing psalms" and the use of the Athanasian Creed in some of the church services caused him much searching of conscience; but when he looked from these things to the work that he had been enabled to accomplish among his poor parishoners he saw there "higher marks of ordination than any man-made articles of subscription." Nevertheless his misgivings were not overcome. The strain that this conflict created resulted in chronic ill-health, and when in 1900 an offer came to him to return to Cambridge as a fellow of his college and vice-principal of Westcott House, "it became evident to all," he says, "that the doctor's verdict must be obeyed and I must give up the college mission work" (*op. cit.*, pp. 143, 145).

During these years the influence of the bishop under whom he served at Monkwearmouth was a dominant factor. "In those earlier years of my life," he writes, looking back over thirty years, "when 'hero-worship' was a second nature to me" (as indeed it continued to be to his life's end), "it was the greatest privilege of all to be allowed to stay with him and go walks with him each afternoon." They talked often of India, which was beginning to cast its spell on Andrews as it had already done on several members of the Westcott family. He remembers that time spent in such company as "golden days," and they were so especially because they were shared with his intimate friend Basil Westcott, who presently left to join the Cambridge Mission at Delhi of which his father had been one of the founders. There were two channels in particular by which, we can see, the influence of this gracious family touched him at this time and moulded his thoughts and plans. One of these was their interest in India, an interest which had already sent three of their sons to serve its people as missionaries, while a fourth, Basil, was about to join them. The other centred in the Gospel of St. John, to the study of which the bishop had devoted his great gifts of insight and scholarship. His interpretation confirmed Andrews in a love of this gospel that throughout his life continued to sustain and inspire him. There was also, he tells us, another "sacred memory" of those early days, associated with the elder sister of his friend Basil, "a frail invalid lady," whose heart was almost more in India with her brother than in England. "In her invalid's room, from which she never went out, the whole living world seemed to be present" (*op. cit.*, p. 134).

These two interests—St John's Gospel and India—which to him appeared to form in certain respects a harmony, continued to hold his heart throughout his whole life. From the time of his conversion onward, this gospel, he tells us, meant more to him than any other part of the New Testament and his references to it in his writings confirm this indebtedness. That the influence of Bishop Westcott had its part in making him so "Johannine" in his Christian outlook cannot be doubted; so also the parallel interest in India that began to lay hold of him at this period was greatly reinforced by his close relation with the Westcotts. His thoughts turned more and more to that land as the sphere for the exercise of his vocation. Thus it came about that, when Basil Westcott died in Delhi of cholera after a very brief period of service as a missionary, this came to him as a personal challenge that could not be set aside. His ties with Pembroke College and Westcott House could not bind him any longer when his friend's death called him. "It was clear to me," he writes, "that I must go out and take his place." On March 20, 1904, which he always, he tells us, looked back to as "a second birthday in his life," he set foot on Indian soil and began his new life in the East (*op. cit.*, pp. 148, 152).

§

Andrews was thirty-three years of age when this second birth came to him. Looking back nearly thirty years later he says that he was one of the "twice-born," so sharply was his life "cut in two" by his entrance into this new environment. That does not mean that there was any break in the continuity and consistency of the two portions. He was aware, he tells us, from his first day in India that he had entered "a different world of human thought," but in spite of this contrast he later on realized the unity that lay beneath. Nor did he himself change. His character and his aims had been already determined and they continued in their course, gaining new hues and new dimensions, but fundamentally the same in their source and their direction. Christ became in India "not less central but more central and more universal; not less divine to me but more so, because more universally human" (*op. cit.*, p. 153).

It is not intended to provide here a full biography of this man but to see him as a great Christian and, just for that reason, as a revolutionary, one who interpreted Christ and Christianity by his acts in such a spirit of devotion and of resolve as to give his life an exceptional significance in the times in which he lived and for the people who took note of him. In the first thirty years the lines of his character had been laid, the sources of his strength had been discovered, the goal of his efforts had been descried. Thenceforward he ran a straight course to the end and lived by one faith. For that reason, once the framework of the thirty strenuous years that remained for him has been outlined, it should be possible to proceed to consider more fully what his life's aims actually were and what was its ultimate achievement.

We have seen that Andrews, as soon as he landed in India, became aware that he had entered a different world of thought from that of his past environment. He had entered as well, as he must soon have realized, a land where a gulf had already begun to open—and was rapidly widening—between the Indian people and their British rulers. The Viceroy, Lord Curzon, was in the last year of his office, and in spite of his great qualities he had a failed to understand India and had only increased the alienation of the two races from each other. G. K. Gokhale, who was the first of the popular leaders to win Andrews's admiration, had withstood the Viceroy in his council with unflinching courage and consummate ability year after year, while other popular leaders, such as Lala Lajpat Rai and B. G. Tilak, were awakening and extending the spirit of rebellion among the common people. Gokhale, reviewing Curzon's seven years of rule after the Viceroy had left India, pointed unerringly to the cause of his tragic failure when he said that he lacked "a sympathetic imagination without which no man can ever understand an alien people."

In St. Stephen's College, Delhi, Andrews was at one of the focal points of this mounting agitation. He was among students, always ready even in Cambridge to harbour insurgent thoughts, and it was not likely that in India such thoughts in those he was brought into contact with would be hid from his discerning eyes. How eager he was to enter into the heritage that India offered him and to understand its genius and appreciate its aspirations was presently revealed in a little book published by him in 1914 called *The Renaissance in India.* There he hails Mahadev Govind Ranade as, by his "largeness of vision and magnanimity of character," one of the chief architects of the India that was then emerging from the shadows. It was peculiarly appropriate that it was Mr Gokhale, disciple of Ranade and heir of his spirit, who launched Andrews in 1913 upon his public career as friend of India and brother of her poor.

In the years from 1904 to 1913 his first duty was to the college in which he taught, and he was not long there before he found even within its walls both friends to bind to himself and evils that had to be redressed. The first of the friends he made there was one, among so many who during his life were granted him, whom he always reckoned and declared to be the most valued and beloved of them all, Sushil Rudra. When Andrews left St. Stephen's College in 1914 Rudra, who was then principal, wrote of him, "No single personality has had so great an influence in the development of the college as Charles Freer Andrews." Andrews could have said no less truly that no single personality had so great an influence upon himself as this friend. "It was an intense joy to me," he says, "to be able to serve under him."

The association of these two men, by the testimony of their colleagues, "largely transformed the college and gave it some of the characteristic features it has since then possessed." It was, indeed, mainly through the efforts of Andrews that Rudra was chosen as principal. This was the first step in a process by which the college divested itself in large measure of its foreignness and became a truly Indian possession, rooted in the soil of the land. The work of collaboration between these two friends proceeded until, by the time Andrews's service at the college came to an end, it possessed a constitution setting it free from many of the limitations that its foreign origin placed upon its influence and granting it what was virtually complete autonomy. What these reforms meant, because of the spirit that they embodied, may be summed up in the testimony of one of his British colleagues, Professor C. B. Young. It fully confirms what, as we have seen, Principal Rudra wrote of him when he left the college. At the time of Andrews's death, in a tribute that he contributed to the college magazine, Mr Young wrote, "Far above particular contributions stands out as his supreme gift to our college his passionate belief in a human brotherhood which overleaps all barriers of race and creed." This was embodied, for example, in the constitution of the college referred to above, with its emphasis on "inter-racial and inter-credal unity." "More than any other man," Mr Young goes on, "he built up that tradition of close personal association between the different communities and races which has been one of the greatest contributions made by St. Stephen's to the national life. His own intimate friendship with Rudra was the starting-point and the incentive of a series of almost innumerable friendships between men of different creeds and races of which the college has been the kindly foster-mother." "Thus a distinctive mark of St. Stephen's College has been the spirit of friendship of which Andrews was supremely the living embodiment" (*see* the articles by Professors Young and Spears in *The Stephanian*, June, 1940).

What was happening to Andrews during these first ten years of his Indian life was that he was testing his powers and gradually discovering the sphere in which they were to be exercised. The milieu of St. Stephen's first gave him his opportunity and he made use of it. He took his place beside his friend Rudra in protesting against the imposition of the

Thirty-Nine Articles and the Athanasian Creed on the young Indian Church, placing upon its neck "a yoke which neither our fathers nor we were able to bear." He fought against sectarian narrowness and came, in consequence, into collision with his bishop, a saint and scholar whom he venerated. Mr Young, though a Baptist missionary, had been invited, largely through the persuasion of Andrews, to become a member of the staff of this Anglican college and had agreed to do so. Andrews's character and his distinguished career as a scholar gave him a dominant influence in college life and he used it to achieve those aims of brotherhood which he felt himself called upon both to extend in their range and to strengthen. He was conscious already of the urgency of the duty that was laid upon him in such matters. Writing of the dominant influence that he exerted in the college, Mr Young makes the comment that "this masterfulness was not due to the self-assertion of egotism (than which nothing could be more unlike Andrews) but to the natural and inescapable prominence of a man who in powers of mind and heart was a giant among pigmies." One more quotation from Mr Young's tribute may complete our view of what he effected in St. Stephen's College, which he never ceased to bear in his heart through all the years given by him to later and larger activities. "All that he thought and said and did in St. Stephen's and outside was the embodiment or application of his commanding passion for unity." This ideal of racial and credal unity furnished "the basal principles of his work in and for India." "He and Rudra in partnership," Mr Young goes on, "made of this place a school of friendship transcending creed and race, a place where, in the phrase of another and even more famous of Andrews's friends 'life is not broken up by narrow domestic walls' " (*op. cit.*, p. 36).

§

The time had arrived, however, when a challenge came to him to exercise in a wider sphere the gift of reconciliation that had been entrusted to him. It was G. K. Gokhale who actually laid this burden upon him, and no one in India could do so with more authority than he. He was the outstanding figure at that time in the public life of his country, a leader, as we can see to-day, of great wisdom and moderation. He may be described as the second in the line of India's liberators during the final stages of her progress towards the status of a free nation. He followed in the steps of M. G. Ranade, to whom he looked up with reverence as the pupil looks up to his teacher, the disciple to his *guru*. The third in that succession, M. K. Gandhi, claims for himself a similar relation to Gokhale. Both Gokhale and Gandhi were engaged at this time in a struggle which to them appeared to concern vitally the honour and self-respect of the Indian people. This was a struggle against the imposition on Indian labourers, under a system of indenture, of what Gokhale described as a "life which, if not one of actual slavery, is at any rate not far removed from it." This system was brought to an end there when in 1917 the government of India stopped all further recruiting, but its consequences still continued and caused intense feeling throughout the land. In 1913 the Viceroy himself expressed "the sympathy of India, deep and burning, . . . and of all lovers of India for their compatriots in South Africa in their resistance to invidious and unjust laws."

The particular instance of this abuse which Mr. Gokhale and Mr. Gandhi were bringing to the notice of the Indian government for redress was that of the Indian "coolies," as they were called, who were recruited for labour in the coal mines of Natal. Gokhale had returned from South Africa, where he had gone to negotiate on behalf of the Indian government, while Gandhi was still there engaged in organizing a movement among the miners demanding justice from South Africa.

It was when matters had reached a crisis and Gandhi was leading the first of his "passive resistance" marches that Gokhale, in November 1913, sent Andrews a telegram inviting him to go out immediately to South Africa "in order to help the Indian community which was suffering from an intolerable wrong." Andrews at once consented, and in January 1914 he arrived in Natal. This was the first of the many journeys in the cause of the oppressed or the unhappy that occupied so much of his life from this time on. Like the "second birth," as he calls it, that came to him at the age of thirty-three, this was a notable hour in his life, when he set himself to a task of emancipation and put away all aims except the fulfilment of his call. It was at this time, apparently, that Albert Schweitzer's example and the message of his book, *The Quest of the Historical Jesus*, came to him, "enkindling," he says, "with fresh ardour [his] drooping heart." He received a new call and took a new decision. "The greatest break in my life came," he writes, "when I decided at last to leave the Cambridge Mission Brotherhood and abandon direct ministerial work under a bishop in order that I might launch out on an unknown sea and set sail for a wider and ampler world" (*What I Owe to Christ*, p. 213). At the same time, in order that he might be in no way encumbered but be ready for "the crisis of a last hour," he not only surrendered his employment but "gave away his life's savings and became a wanderer." His friend Hoyland adds: "I do not think that any of his friends knew how Charlie was supported financially during those strenuous years. . . . He certainly lived on the barest minimum both during the anti-indenture struggle and afterwards" (Hoyland, *C. F. Andrews*, pp. 41, 50).

The anti-indenture struggle—if we include in that description not only the agitation to obtain the abolition of the indenture system itself but also that for the abolition of other evils and injustices that remained as its consequence after it was abolished—occupied a large part of the years that followed upon this first journey; for as David Livingstone crossed and re-crossed Africa to save Africa from slavery, so Andrews crossed and re-crossed the oceans of the world to save the Indian "coolies" from this "near-slavery" which laid its burden of bondage upon them. South Africa, Fiji, the West Indies, British Guiana—these were only some of the lands to which Indians had gone under indenture to work in sugar-plantations or in mines, and wherever there was need of a champion to call attention to injustice done to them or cruelty endured by them Andrews was at their service. Not restlessness but the imperious call of human need sent him posting over land and ocean without rest. He mentions in one place that at the time when he was writing—in 1932—he was on his way to South Africa for the seventh time. His friend H. W. Peet calculated that his book, *What I Owe to Christ*, must have been written "in four out of the five continents and while crossing and re-crossing one or more oceans."

On this first journey he was not alone. His companion—not on this journey only but on several other similar ones as well—was W. W. Pearson, who shared his deep sympathy with the Indian poor as well as his admiration for such distinguished Indians as Rabindranath Tagore. He went with Andrews to South Africa and to the Fiji Islands and thereafter gave himself to work at Santiniketan under the leadership of Tagore. When he died by a fall from a railway train in Italy Andrews suffered, he says, "one of the greatest blows that I had in my life."

On the wharf at Durban the two friends found Gandhi awaiting them. This was Andrews's first meeting with one who thenceforth was to have so great a part in his life. Looking back on it long afterwards, he writes, "Our hearts met from the first moment we saw one another and they have remained united by the strongest ties of love ever since." "To be with him," he goes on, "was an inspiration that awakened all that was best in me and gave me a high courage, enkindled and enlightened by his own" (*What I Owe to Christ*, p. 246). Gandhi had not yet, of course, won for himself the position that as "mahatma" and as the recognized champion of India he held later in the hearts of the Indian people, but he had already shown his willingness to suffer with them and for them. The march of passive protest against injustice that had set out for the Transvaal under his leadership had been broken up, and Gandhi and his wife had been cast into prison at Bloemfontein. By the time that Andrews and Pearson arrived on the scene a temporary accommodation had been arrived at with the South African Government and Gandhi had been released.

During the time spent in South Africa Andrews was making deeper discoveries of what was required of a Christian, and in this Gandhi was by his personality as well as by his acts his chief teacher. He learned with a new conviction two things that remained with him always and shaped the course his life took. One was the conclusion he drew from his observation of Gandhi's character. He tells us, "Even when I was trying to help Mahatma Gandhi at the height of the strain of conflict I was subconsciously occupied in thinking out the meaning of his personality—so entirely 'Hindu' and yet so supremely 'Christian'." The other came from his painful experience of how so many who professed themselves to be Christians and represented the Christian Church treated Gandhi because he did not belong to the white race. "When I reached Natal," he writes, "I found a racial situation within the Church almost exactly parallel to that against which Paul so vehemently contended. . . . I must not for a moment shrink back from the issue but boldly meet it. Like Paul I might have to withstand to their faces those who would bring racialism within the Christian Church" (*op. cit.*, pp. 252, 239, 257). These two standpoints had from this time forward to be his.

In this way his spiritual education was proceeding, and during this period his relation to the Christian Church and especially to the Church of England was exercising his mind. He was not one who shut his eyes to facts, however grim, or hesitated to draw conclusions from them and act accordingly. For that reason, looking back seventeen years later on what he learned during these months, he can speak of "the strain mingled with a buoyant happiness" that this experience under Gandhi's leadership brought to him. Presently, however, news came to him of his beloved mother's death and, a settlement of the Indian question having been reached, he found himself free to visit England. His brief stay there confirmed him in the decision that he could have no more to do with a "colour-ridden Christianity" and must take steps to show that this was so.

On his return to India he took up his residence at Santiniketan—"the Abode of Peace." "The poet," he writes, "in his great-hearted generosity took me just as I was," but, until he had carried his decision into action and surrendered his ministerial status, he felt that he could have no peace of conscience but was living a life of untruth. It is not, of course, to be supposed that he wholly abandoned the Church of England, much less Christianity. He remained "a communicant of the Anglican communion" till his death, but looked upon himself as a layman. "From that day to this," he wrote in his spiritual autobiography, "the thought has been present with me that the true ministry for which I was fitted and prepared by God was prophetic rather than priestly" (*op. cit.*, pp. 268, 270).

Another conflict that made Santiniketan at first less to him than its name signified concerned his attitude to the first great war with Germany that had just burst upon the world. This period of perplexity ended when, to quote his own words, "I saw that I had very nearly betrayed Christ, my Master, when I had allowed the war-fever to get possession of me. Now. . . I was back in my right mind. The relief that came to me with the decision was very great, and it was never regretted afterwards." In this decision, as in so many others, he acknowledges the help given to him both by Tagore and Gandhi. Whether either of them was in the full sense of the word a pacifist is doubtful, but Gandhi's *Satyagraha*—literally "truth-force" but usually taken as equal to "passive-resistance"—and Tagore's ultimate attitude to that war in particular are associated by Andrews in his own case with the authority for him of Christ who, he was confident, "beyond a shadow of doubt," condemned war. "Christ's own war on behalf of the down-trodden peoples all over the world had to be fought and he was calling me to enlist in his service" (*op. cit.*, pp. 276 *ff.*).

Perhaps "the acute inner suffering and trial" that he passed through in this connection was one of the causes of an illness that followed when, in May 1915, he had a severe attack of Asiatic cholera. It appears to have been while he was slowly recovering his strength in Simla that it became "as clear as daylight to him that he was called to go to Fiji to fight in behalf of the Indians employed there under indenture." Not for the first time this summons came to him through a waking dream. At the close of his period at Cambridge he tells how "a moment of luminous vision" enabled him to keep fast hold of unseen realities and remained long with him as a source of spiritual strength. So it was on this occasion also, and on his recovery from his illness he set forth for Fiji under the constraint of this experience.

As on the visit to Africa in the previous year, he was accompanied by William Pearson. This was the first of three visits that he paid to Fiji, the others being in 1917, when he went alone, and in 1936. On the first two occasions his purpose was, as it had been in South Africa, to help those Indians who had gone to Fiji under indenture. His unwearied championship of those suffering under this system did much to expose its evils and to bring about its final abolition—not only in Fiji but in all the British colonies—on January 1, 1920. His third visit was made at the invitation of the Indian community in Fiji in order that he might help them to defend their citizen rights. In the preface to his book, *India and the Pacific*, he gives a summary of his efforts in behalf of the Indians there and in many other parts of the world who were in such great need of a champion. "During the years 1913–1936 I have visited not only Fiji but also nearly all the other colonies where Indians have settled. Everywhere I have received the warmest welcome and have learnt at first hand what handicaps Indians have suffered. Thus a great part of my life has been occupied with these problems."

§

The method that this ambassador felt to be necessary was that of personal contact with those whom he sought to aid. He did not seek to stir up trouble but to allay it, and to do so by such understanding and sympathy as only a full knowledge of each situation could create. So he passed from South Africa to the Fiji Islands, where his method was carefully tested by successive visits. We find him next in East Africa which became—because of its nearness to India, on the one hand, and of the demands that the European settlers were making on the other—the scene of a conflict of critical significance. That was why Srinivasa Sastri, one of the wisest and most patient of India's political leaders, said to Andrews in reference to the struggle for equality of treatment between Indians and Europeans, "If Kenya is lost all is lost." Andrews explains that "if racial discrimination in favour of the white race in Kenya was finally imposed by the Colonial Office no self-respecting Indian could remain within a commonwealth that was nothing more than a sham and a fraud." We see the long shadows from that dispute stretching down to to-day when the question of the "colour bar" is more than ever darkening our skies.

Andrews, accordingly, when he journeyed from colony to colony was an ambassador of inter-racial friendship through the whole world, but especially of an abiding friendship between India and Great Britain. It is difficult to trace his itinerary as he traverses the continents. To protect from injustice Indians settled in British Guiana and British Columbia he found it necessary to visit in person those lands, while the dangerous policy of a "white Australia" sent him to that dominion, whose future, as Andrews realized and as we all realize more clearly than ever to-day, cannot be separated from that of Japan and India. Concluding in 1937 his book *India in the Pacific* he writes, "The Pacific Ocean with its long sea borders and its numberless islands is likely to become at no distant date the centre of fresh prospects for all mankind; and in this process of the ages India with its intellectual and spiritual background will have an important part to play" (p. 206).

It is impossible to do more than name some of those regions to which Andrews's labours in this cause summoned him. From them he returned from time to time to England or to India to have his physical strength renewed or his ardour rekindled. There were other ways of serving India besides placing himself beside the friendless children of her dispersion. He must enter into closer relation with the land itself. It was apparently in London in 1911 that, listening to W. B. Yeats as he read poems of Tagore from the *Gitanjali*, he first became convinced that he must "move amongst the people of India as one of themselves," that he must "be bound up with the life of India in every respect" (*What I Owe to Christ*, p. 267). India had subdued him to herself, and had done so pre-eminently through the ties of affection and reverence that united him with two Indians, Mahatma Gandhi and Rabindranath Tagore.

In what respects these two great Indians influenced him and affected his whole attitude to India will be considered more fully later. Meantime it is to be noted that from the time of his return from his first visit to South Africa in 1914 his home, in any sense in which this world-wanderer can be said to have had a home, was Santiniketan, the home in Bengal of the Bengali poet. It was more than Tagore's personal home, for his father, by taking up his residence there at the close of his career as one of the noble line of theistic reformers of Bengal, had made it a sacred place. An Indian sage was traditionally supposed to retire to such an *ashram* for religious study and meditation when "his hair had grown white and he had seen his son's son." After his father's death Rabindranath Tagore made this place in a wider sense a centre for religious culture and the nucleus of an ambitious dream he cherished of founding an international university. From this place Andrews set out on his errands of mercy across the seas. What it and its master were to him during the last decades of his life can be indicated by two quotations. He tells us that, on his last journey to Fiji, "the memory of the peace of Santiniketan and [Tagore's] home there, where he sat each morning long before the break of day in quiet meditation, was a wonderful comfort in times of utter loneliness and bitter hostility." And again he tells us that, living with him between his voyages, his reverence and love grew deeper year by year. "There at Santiniketan I learned to understand the spiritual beauty which underlies Indian life, keeping it sweet through all the ages in spite of cruelties and wrongs which have gone unredressed" (*op. cit.*, pp. 292, 302).

It was mainly through the medium of these two great Indian personalities—so different in some of their fundamental outlooks upon life but so united in their devotion to their common motherland and to what they believed to affect her honour—that Andrews looked at India and appraised her greatness. Through them and others of their quality he would have foreigners see India and recognize (as he says) her "inner moral beauty." The ties of reverence and affection that bound him to them bound him to India. Andrews accompanied Tagore in 1916 to China and Japan and was with him in Great Britain and in America on other occasions, but it was the peace of Santiniketan and the poet's own "serene and beautiful spirit" that made him look forward from his arduous wanderings "with a fond and eager joy" to his return there. "A quiet haven had been entered," he says, "and the vessel of my life found its anchorage" (*Christ in the Silence*, pp. 18, 20–21).

The demands that Gandhi made upon him were usually of another sort. The contemplative needs of his nature found what they needed in the Abode of Peace and in the fellowship it offered; but he could not long remain inactive and he must be at Gandhi's side exercising *Satyagraha* along with him; or watching over him as he by his fasts staked his life on the justice of his cause; or again, beside him in London supporting him at the round-table conferences. These two mentors represented two sides of his nature, both of which needed to be satisfied, and we may conclude that during the years of alternating action and contemplation the *ashram* of Gandhi and the *ashram* of Tagore found an equilibrium that brought to him fulfilment.

Nor does that sum up the duties that sent him during the busy and troubled years "between the wars" on errands of mercy to the ends of India and of the earth. It might be earthquake or flood or famine or clashes on the North-West Frontier or the last sickness of a single forlorn Indian student in Germany,—this "brother of the poor" could not shut his ears to the call. He must be up and away,

> *Doing the King's work all the dim day long,*
> *In his old coat. . . .*
> *Smoked like a herring, dining on a crust.*

But as the crowded years went past and his strength grew less his still unwearied spirit had to find other means than those of travel by which to serve his fellow men. His pen had never been inactive at any time, but when he found it necessary to seek more often the quiet of Santiniketan or Selly Oak or Pembroke College he used the opportunity in new ways. It is true that his spiritual autobiography, *What I Owe to Christ,* was written in the midst of many journeyings—as he says, "in the midst of the struggle rather than in retirement and retreat"—but other books that followed and were written with the same aim were, it is evident, the product of times of enforced leisure and the fruit of a desire to strengthen young people especially "in their faith and love for Christ."

Thus his labours for his fellow men of every land continued and expanded. His appeals, whether these were made by his acts or by his pen, issued always from a heart overflowing with an affection that was personal and, indeed, individual in its direction and that was glad and even gay. So when he lay dying in hospital in Calcutta he was still, as ever, "surrounded by an atmosphere of love, joy and inward peace." There, on April 4, 1940, this good soldier of Jesus Christ obtained his discharge and his voyagings their end.

2

Friend of India

THERE are three aspects of C. F. Andrews's life and his achievements that deserve to be more closely studied, for the message that they "placard" before the modern world and the example that they show to it. These may be represented by three titles that describe what he was and the kind of service that he set himself to render to his fellows. He was pre-eminently a friend, overflowing in his friendship and fellowship with men, and especially he was a friend of India. That he was that in India in his relations with men of every class and creed and colour, no one can deny. The other two titles of honour that were bestowed on him were tributes paid by the multitude in India who loved him and watched him at work there. It was Gandhi that first gave him the designation *Dinbandhu*, which means "Brother of the Humble" and suggests many enterprises of help for the despised and the suffering that draw him like a magnet. He was also frequently described by Christian Indians and, more significantly still, by non-Christians, reinterpreting his initials, as "Christ's Faithful Apostle." He was probably right when he said of himself that the ministry for which he was fitted and prepared was prophetic and not priestly; that it was, if we may express the distinction from another point of view, dynamic and not static. But, as the word prophet has its associations with the Old Testament rather than the New, he may more fitly be described as "an apostle," and an apostle of the order of his most beloved teacher, St. John.

Through these three aspects of his service of mankind runs the silken cord of friendship holding them together and giving to them a peculiar sheen. He was first and last a friend. In India they have a name which means "Friend of

All the World," *Jagad-mitra*, and surely there was never anyone to whom it would have been more aptly given than to Andrews. But his was not a vague cosmopolitanism; his friendship had, as all friendships to be real must have, a centre: or we might more truly say, two centres—one a centre of reception and the other a centre of distribution. Of the source from which his great power of affection was derived we must speak later, for to leave that out would be to leave all out. But from him radiated forth a warmth that kindled a responsive glow, like a household fire, in hearts and homes wherever he went, but that glowed nowhere more comfortingly than in the land that itself so conquered him. "I longed," he says, "to be bound up with the life of India in every respect, . . . to be among them as one of themselves, and not an alien and a foreigner." The range of that affection was unlimited. He was a friend of India first: but he was at the same time a "friend of all the world."

That is the primary fact that has to be realized in regard to Andrews. In the capacity for friendship he was unique. He had other great qualities without which this central source of strength would have been inadequate to the tasks he undertook and accomplished. But here lay the citadel of his personality, and of its range and power we have to be convinced if we are to do him justice. Professor T. G. P. Spear, one of his British colleagues in St. Stephen's College, writes of him: "Andrews' life was a catalogue of friendships; each stage is marked by a new friend, each one, as he would characteristically say, dearer than a brother. His capacity for new friendships remained fresh to the last and while he was constantly making new friends he never lost an old one" (*The Stephanian*, June 1940, p. 4). That is a remarkable testimony but it is confirmed by all we know of him. If each friend he made was "characteristically" described by him as "dearer than a brother," is there not exaggeration in these professions? One remembers how Martin Luther said that the dearest of his children was the one that was at the moment on his knee. So it was, it would seem, with Andrews. When in his thought and imagination he summoned one of his friends before him, his whole heart warmed and glowed, as Luther's did. Was he, then, a sentimentalist? Here is what Professor Spear says of his work as a peacemaker in labour disputes: "On the surface it seemed as though the gentle sentimentalist had little chance in bargaining with hard-boiled industrialists and matter-of-fact officials, but when they met it was the prophet in homespun who was fit to get the better of the men of the world. His intellect retained the keen edge of its Cambridge days, his memory was a store-house of facts and he added to both an intense perception of broad moral issues. To the innocence of the dove he united the wisdom of the serpent and the unexpected combination often produced inspiring results" (*op. cit.*, p. 20).

To a reader of his books Andrews's expression of his affection may sometimes seem so unrestrained as to sound exaggerated, but when his words are tested by his deeds there can be no doubt of their sincerity. No one can be dismissed as a sentimentalist whose emotion proceeds at once to action and finds its fulfilment in unswerving purpose. When he was converted he set himself at once—"almost next day," he says—to the service of the poor and the ignorant round about him in Birmingham and in the college mission at Walworth, and so it was wherever he might be all his life long. As he himself says, "a fugitive and cloistered virtue" never had any attraction for him. He believed, in words that he often quotes, that "love's strength standeth in love's sacrifice." A word of Christ's that evidently meant much to him—and that was given to him, he tells us, by his father—was, "Ye are my friends, if ye do whatsoever I command you," and his emphasis is placed upon the doing. Some lines quoted in the memorial appeal issued by his

Indian friends after his death from a poem by Andrews himself reveal how central this union of emotion and duty was in his religion:

> "'*Who loveth much'—the Master gave the meed,*
> *Not by the rule of indolent belief,*
> *Not by professing sympathy with grief*
> *Without the act. Nay, by the living deed*
> *He fixed for man Love's everlasting creed.*"

This was his "everlasting creed" and to make it real once more as it had been in the early centuries was one of his most significant services to his time.

The scene that he chose, or rather that was chosen for him, for this demonstration was India. He became, in a sense true of no other foreigner, a friend of India. But India was not for him an abstraction: she was men and women and children of every class and kind, and the way to their hearts, as he himself repeatedly emphasizes, was opened for him through his friendship with his first Indian friend, Sushil Rudra. As a result of his own experience he was always urging upon those who desired to understand and to serve the people of India that they should have one or two Indian friends whom they could grapple to themselves. Because of the intimacy of his relation with Rudra "the first newness of India," he says, "passed into closest contact with its people." "Many have greatly wondered how I came so quickly to understand the people of India and to be understood by them. The answer is quite simple and the secret is easily told. Such a close friend as Sushil Rudra is very rarely given in this life to any man" (*What I Owe to Christ*, pp. 157, 161). He repeatedly tells us indeed that of all his many friends Rudra was the dearest. We have seen that he took a leading part in securing the appointment of his friend as the first Indian principal of St. Stephen's College. It was largely through his insight and his freedom from all self-interest that Sushil Kumar Rudra was chosen for this position for which he was eminently fitted, and so the custom of reserving it for an Englishman was abandoned. St. Stephen's has never had reason to regret the course it then took, and Andrews by this act had set his foot on the road of India's vindication along which he was to travel so far in the years to come.

But notable as was his friendship for Rudra, and fruitful as was that early relationship in moulding his whole future course, it is with two great non-Christian Indians, the greatest of their time, that Andrews is associated in the eyes of the world, and it was above all through his fellowship with them that he both received from India and gave to India what made him India's friend and helper. These were Mahatma Gandhi and Rabindranath Tagore. With these two men, so different in their gifts but so representative each in his own way, of India at her highest, Andrews maintained, all through his career from the time when he left St. Stephen's College onwards, an intimacy which neither their engrossing tasks nor his distant journeyings were able to disturb, and one which they prized no less than he. To have kept this close fellowship fully alive and active with so much acknowledged profit on both sides through so long a time was in itself a remarkable achievement, especially so when it was a relationship that had to overcome both racial differences and the hostility that conflicting national interests might arouse. That this was achieved is itself a convincing evidence of the high spiritual quality of these men, each so remarkable in his own nature and gifts.

§

To tell the story of Andrews's relations with Gandhi is to tell the story of India's political struggles during the last twenty-five years. That story cannot be told in any detail here but only as it reveals the mind and heart of Andrews and the significance of the life he lived in India's service. The two men (almost of the same age) felt themselves at once akin, and a partnership was inaugurated which had notable consequences for each of them and for the country to which they had already dedicated their lives. Andrews has described the meeting at Durban at Easter 1914 and its effect upon himself. "Our hearts," he writes, "met from the first moment we saw each other, and they have remained united by the strongest ties of love ever since. To be with him was an inspiration which awakened all that was best in me and gave me a high courage, enkindled and enlightened by his own. His tenderness towards every slightest thing that suffered pain was only a part of his tireless search for truth whose other name was God" (*op. cit.*, p. 246).

It is not so easy to estimate how far Andrews on his part may have influenced Gandhi and modified his policies. To read the enigma of the Mahatma's character and pronounce any judgement on his career can hardly be attempted with any confidence as yet. At the same time some of the qualities that make him so great a figure can be recognized and the strong attraction that Andrews felt to him fully understood. Of the depth of his compassion for the poor and the downtrodden in his own land—and, indeed, as Andrews says, "for every slightest thing that suffered pain"—there can be no dispute, and that would be matched by a similar compassion in Andrews's heart. There has been much compassion in India from the days of Buddha onwards, but a compassion that flies from pain rather than, as it was in the case of these two mahatmas, that takes it upon the heart and strives to heal it. Another quality that is unmistakable in Gandhi is his courage, and we have seen already that, with all his gentleness, Andrews was by no means lacking in that either.

Andrews, in a passage just quoted, describes one of the

sources of the inspiration that Gandhi awakened in him as "his tireless search for truth." Here also one must agree that the claim is justified. Gandhi must be recognized to have constantly sought to build upon a foundation of reality, and, still more evidently, to have been wholly sincere and honourable in his dealings. Compassion and courage and fundamental truthfulness are qualities of nobility that can hardly be surpassed in their significance for any man and especially for a politican, and they justify the title of Mahatma, or Great Soul, that India has bestowed upon its leader. It is not to be wondered at that Andrews's kindred spirit should greet in him such moral greatness.

Gandhi was scarcely less grateful to Andrews for what this friendship meant to him. Thus, after Andrews's death, he recorded in his organ *Harijan* how close the bond between them was. "Nobody probably knew Charlie Andrews as well as I did," he wrote. "Gurudev [Tagore] was *guru*—master—to him. When we met in South Africa we simply met as brothers and remained as such to the end. There was no distance between us. It was not a friendship between an Englishman and an Indian. It was an unbreakable bond between two seekers and servants." That need not imply that they were in all respects in full agreement. For example, Gandhi's asceticism and some of the consequences that followed from it in his policy and his public acts Andrews seems to have sometimes frankly opposed and criticised. This was one of the respects in which he was more in accord with "the less puritan ideals of Santiniketan" (*Mahatma Gandhi's Ideas*, p. 331). In this respect, as in others, Gandhi represents the Hindu tradition, with its negation of life and life's rewards. What counterbalanced for Andrews this defect in Gandhi was "an amazing sweetness and child-like innocence" that he found in him and that makes him trace "an illuminating parallel with Francis of Assisi." "I could easily imagine Gandhi preaching to the birds," he writes, and as a matter of fact one whom we may call a spiritual ancestor of Gandhi, Tukaram, a very gracious poet saint of three centuries earlier, gathered the birds about himself in this very fashion. Tukaram and Gandhi represent, indeed, the flower of one strain in Hinduism, but Andrews was "brought up against inassimilable features also" (*op. cit.*, p. 344).

One of these "inassimilable features" was Gandhi's "fasts unto death," announced by him as such in 1932 and 1939, to which Andrews seems to have been strongly opposed. That "terrible phrase," he calls it, "which seems to me morally repulsive"; and for a time, at least, Gandhi appears to have recognized that such a method of bringing about his aim of "converting the hearts of Englishmen" would not prove successful. "It is easy," Andrews wrote to him, "to get their sympathy with the removal of untouchability"; but "it is *not* easy to get sympathy with the idea of committing suicide by fasting unto death. The horror and repulsion are too great." Gandhi was willing to admit that "it looks certainly barbarous," but this did not prevent him from announcing yet another fast of this kind five years later.[1] His less drastic fasts, such as the one for twenty-one days at Delhi in 1924 he viewed differently. That fast was undertaken for his self-purification: in Gandhi's own words, "the prayer of a bleeding heart for forgiveness for sins unwittingly committed." He felt himself involved in the guilt of the terrible outbreaks of violence that followed upon one of his non-co-operation experiments. To Andrews he seemed to be "bearing the sins and sorrows of his people," but "to put his life in the scales" as he did when he announced that he would "fast unto death" went, in Andrews's opinion, beyond anything that he had a right to do (*op. cit.*, p. 308).

There were other matters on which they were in sharp

[1] These quotations are from letters written in 1933 and from *Harijan*, April 15 of that year.

disagreement, when neither of them was willing to give way to the other. One of these was the burning of foreign cloth.[1] Their relation to each other is vividly revealed in their arguments on this subject, and Andrews's letter, as given by Gandhi in the weekly paper *Young India*, deserves to be quoted in full.

> "I know," he wrote, "that your Burning of Foreign Cloth is with the idea of helping the poor, but I feel that you have gone wrong. There is a subtle appeal to racial feeling in that word 'foreign' which day by day appears to need checking and not fomenting. The picture of your lighting that great pile, including delicate fabrics, shocked me intensely. We seem to be losing sight of the great outside world to which we belong and concentrating selfishly on India; and this must (I fear) lead back to the old, bad, selfish nationalism. If so, we get into the vicious circle from which Europe is trying so desperately to escape. But I cannot argue it out. I can only say again that it shocked me, and seemed to me a form of violence; and yet I know how violence is abhorrent to you. I do not at all like this question of foreign cloth being made into a religion.
>
> "I was supremely happy when you were dealing giant blows at the fundamental moral evils—drunkenness, drug-taking, untouchability, race arrogance, etc., and when you were, with such wonderful and beautiful tenderness, dealing with the hideous vice of prostitution. But lighting bonfires of foreign cloth and telling people that it is a religious sin to wear it; destroying in the fire the noble handiwork of one's own fellow men and women, of one's own brothers and sisters abroad, saying it would be 'defiling' to use it—I cannot tell you how different it appears to me! Do you know I almost

[1] This seems to have been about 1921.

> fear to wear now the *khaddar* that you have given me, lest I should appear to be judging other people, as a Pharisee would, saying, 'I am holier than thou!' I never felt like this before.
>
> "You know how, when anything that you do hurts me, I must cry out to you, and this has hurt me."

Gandhi's comment on this letter indicates once more how close was the intimacy between them. "Whenever he feels hurt over anything I have done," he writes, "(and this is by no means the first of such occasions) he deluges me with letters without waiting for an answer. For it is love speaking to love, and not arguing." But Gandhi was not to be easily moved when he had made up his mind. He goes on: "I remain just as convinced as ever of the necessity of burning." Yet another instance of divergence in their convictions is seen in regard to questions relating to war and Gandhi's inconsistent attitude in encouraging recruiting for the first world war. He found himself, he says, "in painful disagreement" with his friend but he could not convince him in this case any more than in the other that what he was doing was contrary to the spirit of *Ahimsa* (*Mahatma Gandhi's Ideas*, pp. 133, 146).

§

Two of the principles that guided Gandhi and that in theory—though not always in Gandhi's application of them—were accepted with enthusiasm by Andrews are what are called *Ahimsa* and *Satyagraha*. The essential harmony between his mind and Gandhi's is due to their agreement in what these two "practical religious ideals" of Gandhi signified for Gandhi himself and the reinforcement that they brought to Andrews in his labour in the cause of India (*op. cit.*, Caps. VII, XIII).

Ahimsa is a Sanskrit word with a long religious history

which implies abstinence from inflicting injury on any sentient being, and for the most part it has been understood in that negative sense. Thus for the followers of the Jain religion, as well as for many Hindus, the often quoted sentence "Ahimsa is the highest religious duty (*dharma*)" has a limited ethical range. But for Gandhi, as he tells us, "it has a world of meaning and takes me into realms much higher, infinitely higher." Gandhi was not the first in India so to deepen and enlarge the significance of the word. Mahadev Govind Ranade, the reform leader, who was, as we have seen, Gokhale's *guru*, equated Ahimsa with love, just as Gandhi does, and in the Hindu theistic tradition called *Bhakti*—to which both Ranade and Gandhi belonged—such an interpretation would not be strange and such an ideal was not infrequently proclaimed. But as Gandhi knew, and indeed discovered from his own experience (when, for example, he mercifully destroyed a suffering calf), his interpretation of the word often aroused violent opposition and anger among orthodox Hindus.

Satyagraha goes along with Ahimsa in Gandhi's philosophy. It is a word—apparently coined by himself—which means "truth force" or perhaps rather "holding to truth." He explains a Satyagraha-struggle as a "fight on behalf of truth consisting chiefly in self-purification and self-reliance." He often translates it also as "soul-force." Along with Ahimsa it implies a programme of what is often called "non-violent non-co-operation," though that description hardly conveys its positive character. It was a weapon such as had often been resorted to in the West as well as in the East when the weak have had to face the strong. Gandhi himself tells us how it first came to him. "It was the New Testament," he is reported as saying in his early years in South Africa, "which really awakened me to the rightness and value of passive resistance. The *Bhagavadgita* deepened the impression and Tolstoy's *The Kingdom of Heaven is*

Within You gave it a permanent form" (quoted in *Renascent India*, by H. C. E. Zacharias, p. 77).

How deeply religious this Ahimsa-Satyagraha teaching was, as Gandhi interpreted it, and how central in determining his actions, can be seen clearly from a passage which Andrews quotes in his *Mahatma Gandhi's Ideas* (pp. 225 *f.*). Gandhi is writing, apparently, in 1920, and referring to "the non-co-operation struggle in order to right the Khilafat and the Punjab wrongs and to win *swaraj.*" This is what he calls his *Dharma Yuddha* or "War of Religion."

> "My confidence," he says, "is unshaken that, if a single satyagrahi [that is, follower of Satyagraha] holds out to the end victory is certain. This is the beauty of Satyagraha. It comes up to us; we have not to go out in search for it. There is a virtue inherent in the principle itself. A war of righteousness in which there are no secrets to be guarded, no scope for cunning and no place for untruth, comes unsought, and a man of religion is ever ready for it. . . . A war of righteousness can be waged only in the name of God and it is only when the satyagrahi feels quite helpless, when he is apparently on his last legs and finds utter darkness all around him, that God comes to his rescue. God helps us when we feel ourselves to be humbler than the very dust under our feet. Only to the weak and helpless is divine succour vouchsafed."

The fact that Gandhi sees himself always waging a religious war, which this passage makes evident, awakens suspicion of him in many minds. They may admire his self-dedication to his aim, but they are aware of a danger that lies in the very intensity of his beliefs. For Andrews, on the contrary, these facts awaken his reverence. Even when he disagrees with Gandhi he is conscious that Gandhi has reached the conclusions which he holds so strongly by arguments "that have been tested and examined in his personal experience by his own pure spirit," and therefore no more can be said. "No saint," says Mr H. N. Brailsford of Gandhi in *Subject India*, "has ever lived his creed more faithfully." That is a tribute of the highest order, and it can be paid no less truly to Andrews's fidelity to his creed. If the two creeds were closely similar—as they in considerable measure appear to be—then no more would need to be said, but perhaps Andrews was deliberately silent in regard to some of the differences that were indeed there all the time because their agreement was of so much greater significance in the circumstances of the struggle Gandhi was waging for his country's freedom. That was what mattered supremely at the moment.

Yet he can say with no reservation as he looks back years afterwards at what Gandhi did in South Africa, "He had then put us Christians to shame; and his example had ever since set me seriously thinking. What he called Satyagraha or Truth Force was obviously Christian; while the savage brutality of war was the reverse" (*What I Owe to Christ*, p. 277).

There was another aspect of Gandhi's character that bound Andrews to him no less closely than did his faithfulness to Ahimsa and Satyagraha—his compassion for the poor. He rejoices to see Tagore and Gandhi more fully at one in this matter than in any other. They both hold strongly "that God is to be found among the lowliest children of the soil." Andrews tells us in one place how, one evening while he was with Gandhi at their devotions in Gandhi's *ashram* at Sabarmati, Ghandhi asked him to read a poem by Tagore and he read the poem that begins with the words, "Here is Thy footstool and there rest Thy feet, where live the poorest and lowliest and lost." He goes on: "It seemed to me that in that company of Mahatma Gandhi and his chosen band of followers the presence of God was almost visibly near at hand in the cool of the day there in that *ashram* where the poor were so loved and revered. Long years afterwards I heard Mahatma in a deeply moving way refer to that evening worship and that reading from Rabrindranath Tagore, and realized that he had felt, as I had on that occasion, the mysterious presence of the Eternal."

It was such deep elements of agreement in their attitude to life and its duties that made the relationship between Andrews and Gandhi so intimate and their harmony so close. The materials are not available that would enable us to estimate with any exactness the part that Andrews played in "the long, slow agony" of the as yet unfinished struggle for India's political emancipation. In that struggle the personality of Gandhi far more than anything else determined—and still determines—India's attitude. Andrews believed without reserve in the spirit that guided Gandhi in his struggle; it was in the main the same as that which guided himself. His primary concern was to see to it that the war for India's independence was maintained at a consistently high moral level. He quotes in one place words of Gandhi himself in which he describes Tagore as "a sentinel warning us against the approach of enemies called Bigotry, Lethargy, Ignorance and other members of that brood." Andrews could no less truly be called a sentinel, though the enemies that he kept at bay might bear other names. His championship of India's cause in South Africa when the summons first came to him was a championship of such a kind, and his outlook upon the distresses of India and of the world in its essentials never changed. He saw, writ large in India's relation with Great Britain, the moral evil of subjection. He had seen this evil at its acutest in the case of Indians settled in British colonies or dominions, and he found much the same situation within India itself. Foreign domination, there, as elsewhere, "creates in the rulers a domineering spirit and implants in the ruled a subservience that destroys all moral standards. Race feeling with bitterness on both sides becomes intensified" (*Britain and India*, p. 92).

In all these moral aims that were of the first consequence for him in determining political strategy he found himself able to support Mr Gandhi. "I can trace every day more clearly," he says, "how this prolonged subjection to a foreign rule is injuring something vital in [India's] soul" (*op. cit.*, p. 65). Looking at the problems of India and the sorrows of her poor peasantry as well as the eager demands for freedom of those who felt themselves to be in bondage and despised, he says, "No doubt if I had been born in India and had passed through all those difficult years I should speak exactly as Mahatma Gandhi does." Sometimes we may feel that he surrenders too much of his critical faculty in his desire to identify himself with a people whose cause he believes in and whose poverty and distress he sees so vividly, but his deepest conviction was that what was needed in India was "to set the moral value of things right," and it is certainly true, as he claims, that "Gandhi has done more than any other living soul to bring this new moral emphasis into prominence" (*op. cit.*, p. 153).

For these reasons Andrews was always ready to give to Gandhi the sympathy and comradeship that meant to much to him. What actual assistance in political action he rendered we cannot be sure. Gandhi tells us how when he issued an open letter "giving concrete shape to the Khilafat claims" his "revisionists were Rudra and Andrews," and how "non-co-operation was conceived and hatched under Rudra's hospitable roof" (*Mahatma Gandhi's Ideas*, p. 99). No doubt Andrews would be there and we know that he was in full sympathy with that particular policy. But it was much more for his affection and encouragement in times of suffering and crisis that Andrews's personal presence was desired by Gandhi and his support valued. His home in India—in so far as this wanderer can be said to have had a home there or anywhere—was at Santiniketan, but when a cry for help came to him from Gandhi he never failed to respond. "This was especially the case," he says, "when he [Gandhi] had any dangerous illness. On two such occasions—in the year 1918 and in 1924—I was with him night and day while he was very near death" (*op. cit.*, p. 18). In 1924 he was with him both while recovering from the operation that he had to undergo while he was in prison in Poona and also when, later in the year, he undertook a twenty-one days' fast at Delhi, "as an act of penance on behalf of the sins and infirmities of his own people." The special sin for which the Mahatma undertook this act of vicarious suffering was that of Hindu-Muslim antagonism and for a while it seemed as if this heroic effort at conciliation might succeed. But the high hopes that were at first aroused were not fulfilled. "Evils," Andrews writes, "that are centuries old cannot altogether be overcome by a single act" (*op. cit.*, p. 319). That fatal fissure within the unity of the life of India remains unhealed, and still prevents her full attainment of the status of a free nation.

Again when Gandhi went to London in September, 1930, for one more of the efforts to bring about a solution of the Indian problem, Andrews was there with him, acting we may say, as a liaison officer between the two lands both of which he loved and whose reconciliation he so much desired. Once more there was failure. But though the same failure has been repeatedly experienced since then Andrews as long as he lived neither slackened his efforts in the cause of India nor weakened in his confidence in the achievement of the aims that for him were embodied in the person of Mohandas Gandhi. Gandhi tells us that he said to him on the bed from which he was never to rise, "Mohan, *swaraj* is coming."

In the last years before the end came to his long campaign Andrews was more in England and less in India than he had been in the preceding twenty years. In one of the books of devotion that in these later years occupied his attention alongside of the cause of India he can still bear witness to the nearness to his heart of Gandhi and what Gandhi represented. "Mahatma Gandhi though absent in India," he writes in the preface to his book *Christ in the Silence*, "has been very near in spirit to me, both by his letters and personal friendship. He has interpreted, through his actions, much that I have tried to write about at first hand in this task. For in ways often difficult to understand but amazing in their supreme sacrifice he has shown me the meaning of that 'greater love' whereof Christ speaks, when a man lays down his life for his friend." There could hardly be a greater tribute than that to this friendship which bound Andrews not only to Gandhi but also to the cause of liberty and peace, of Ahimsa and Satyagraha, which in his eyes Gandhi so supremely represented.

Gandhi evidently hoped that what he calls "Andrews's legacy" might be a renewed effort to reconcile India and England. "Not one of the heroic deeds of Andrews," he wrote after his death, "will be forgotten so long as England and India live. If we really love Andrews's memory we may not have hate in us for Englishmen of whom Andrews was among the best and noblest. It is possible, quite possible, for the best Englishmen and the best Indians to meet together and never to separate till they have evolved a formula acceptable to both. The legacy left by Andrews is worth the effort. That is the thought that rules me whilst I contemplate the divine face of Andrews and what innumerable deeds of love he performed so that India may take her independent place among the nations of the earth" (*Harijan*, April 19, 1940).

§

But Gandhi's great gift to Andrews of his friendship and the contagion of his passionate purpose in the service of

India must not stand by itself as interpreting Andrews's secret to us. There must be placed beside it the great debt—complementary in large measure to the other—that he owed to Rabindranath Tagore. One sometimes asks oneself the question, To which was he indebted most? But perhaps Andrews himself could not have answered. Each contributed something to him that he needed and that he valued greatly: the one what we may describe in Andrews's own words as "that stress upon action that comes from crisis"; the other the need for peace, the peace of Santiniketan, the Abode of Peace. He loved them both, but of Tagore he always speaks, not with love alone but with reverence.

Between these two friends of Andrews there was a contrast that was superficial but at the same time deeply significant. The fundamental harmony that overcame the discords was due to their common devotion to India and to the heritage of Hindu culture which they possessed so fully and valued so highly. But their homes were separated by the whole breadth of India and they spoke different languages. The one, Tagore, was an internationalist and a humanist; the other, Gandhi, was a nationalist, not in the sense of having any antagonism to other nations, but in that of what he called *Swadeshi* ("I confine my attention to the land of my birth"), and he was also an ascetic. Gandhi again must be described as a politician, while Tagore writes of himself, "I pray that I may never die a patriot or a politician but as a free spirit; not as a journalist but as a poet" (*Letters from a Friend*, p. 168).

One could go on accumulating antitheses in regard to the two men and yet at the end we would have to admit that their agreement was nearer to the truth about them than their divergence, the essential harmony than their superficial discord. Between them they go far to represent the real unity that behind all differences makes India one nation. Andrews was fortunate in having grappled so close to himself two such representatives of India's infinite variëty.

Tagore had his spiritual descent from Raja Ram Mohan Roy, that great herald of the dawn in India of whom Indians, looking back to his shining figure leading his people forward in the early years of the nineteenth century, could fitly say in the words of Emerson, "He first cut the cable and gave us a chance at the dangers and the glories of blue water." His father, Devendranath Tagore, the *Maharshi* or "Great Sage" as he was called, has a place only less significant in India's spiritual emancipation. His autobiography Evelyn Underhill ranks with "the few classic autobiographies bequeathed to us by certain of the mystics and saints." His son, Satyendranath, describes it in his introduction as "a record of the struggle of a soul striving to rise from empty idolatrous ceremonial to the true worship of the living God." The Maharshi was an Indian theist and could say, "The Nirvana-ṣalvation of the Upanishads did not find a place in my heart" (*The Autobiography of Maharshi Devendranath Tagore*, p. 165). "Seekers after God," he says in another place, "must realize Brahma in these three places. They must see Him within, see Him without and see Him in the abode of Brahma where he exists in Himself. When we see Him within our soul we say, 'Thou are the innermost soul of the soul; thou art my Father, thou art my Friend, thou art my Comrade.' When we see Him without us we say, 'Thy royal throne is in the infinite sky.' When we see Him in Himself, see the supreme Truth in His own sanctuary, then we say, 'Thou art in thine own Self supreme Goodness and Peace; One without a second' " (*op. cit.*, p. 150).

That was the heritage into which Rabindranath Tagore entered, which helped to make him the poet and the deeply religious man that Andrews revered and loved. He could not but be a world citizen but he lived in an age of nationalism when love for his own land and people seemed of necessity to set him at variance with many who passed India by or depised her. In his letters the resentment that this arouses is constantly being expressed. "Ram Mohan Roy," he writes in a letter to Andrews from New York, "was the first great man in our age who had the profound faith and large vision to feel in his heart the unity of soul between the East and the West. I follow him though he is practically rejected by my countrymen" (*Letters to a Friend*, p. 109). One of the minor conflicts and irritations that arose between Tagore and Gandhi was caused by Gandhi's depreciation of Ram Mohan Roy as "a pigmy" compared with the more "swadeshi" saints Kabir and Nanak, who owed nothing to the West. "If he is not understood by modern India," Tagore sorrowfully recognized, "this only shows that the pure light of her own truth has been obscured for the moment by the storm-clouds of passion." "The idea of non-co-operation unnecessarily hurts that truth. It is not our hearth-fire but the fire that burns out our hearth and home" (*op. cit.*, pp. 165, 163).

Thus there was a deep division in his soul, a wound that could not be healed and that carried continual pain into his heart. He could not "tune his mood of mind to be in accord with the feeling of excitement sweeping across the country." A voice says to him, "Your place is on the 'seashore of worlds' with children; there is your peace and I am with you there." He can recognize the value of what Gandhi was doing, "calling up the immense power of the meek that has been waiting in the heart of the destitute and insulted humanity of India" (*op. cit.*, pp. 129, 128). He recognized its value and its necessity but he had to remain outside of it all.

So he does not appear to a reader of the *Letters to a Friend* as he appeared to that friend himself, the messenger of peace, the dispenser of "calm wisdom." The same disquiet sounds through these letters as we hear in Amiel's *Journal*, and behind what we may in both cases describe as this buddhistic undernote of restlessness there is a deep longing for peace, but seldom, except in nostalgic memory, its attainment. He calls it the shadow of his own egotism, and the psychological insight of many of his spiritual ancestors among the poet saints of India diagnosed in themselves the same disease. When Andrews speaks of "his serene and beautiful spirit" we must suppose that in Santiniketan the peace they both so often longed for indeed abode, but we find it easier to recognize Tagore's chief role in Andrews's description of him as "the great Sentinel on guard for the integrity of his country."

We can see Andrews turning from one to another of these two men, entering with full understanding into the spirit of each and seeking to hold together the two halves of truth that between them they represent. He found the harmonizing element in "the universal principle of Ahimsa" to which both these great Indians equally adhered, and which Gandhi sought to keep at the centre of the national movement. The difference between them in temperament and outlook, that he was constantly seeking to harmonize for the good of the India they both desired so much to serve, evidently had a great, and sometimes a painful, interest for him. In *Mahatma Gandhi's Ideas* (p. 343) he quotes a suggestion of Romain Rolland that Tagore is the Plato of our time and Gandhi the St. Paul. With the second parallel he is in agreement to this extent, that Gandhi experienced "a great upheaval of conscience such as we imply by the word conversion," and further that Gandhi had a strong sense of sin and could cry like the Apostle, "Unhappy man that I am, who shall deliver me from the body of this death?" The parallel between Tagore and Plato evidently appeared to him to be nearer the truth, for, he says, "there is in Tagore all the catholicity and the passionate love of ideal, spiritual beauty which the name of Plato connotes." He goes on: "There is much more also: and I have seen in Tagore that which his own wonderful countenance portrays, the serenity which is found in the Gospel picture of Christ. No one has taught me more of that divine character than Rabindranath Tagore has done by his own life and example."

Quite evidently, as has been already suggested, Tagore in Andrews's eyes stood for serenity and peace and his home, Santiniketan, beckoned to him from across the seas as indeed the Abode of Peace. But to read Tagore's letters to Andrews and Pearson hardly confirms this view of him. We see him there on almost every page as a man deeply divided in spirit by a conflict that his time and its problems had created within him. "My India," he writes to Andrews, "is an idea, not a geographical expression. Therefore I am not a patriot —I shall ever seek my compatriots all over the world. You are one of them and I am sure that there are many others. My solitary cell is awaiting me in my motherland. In their present state of mind they will have no patience with me who believe God to be higher than my country" (*Letters to a Friend*, p. 123). So it is he rather than Gandhi who cries, "Unhappy man that I am," and who, in the spirit of St. Paul, could even say, "My heart's desire and prayer to God for India is that she may be saved," or, as he would rather put it, "that she may understand the true meaning of emancipation."

§

It would be foolish to attempt to assess the value of the contribution that each of these two remarkable personalities made to Andrews's understanding of India and to his vivid appreciation of her distresses and her demands. He rejoiced in what each gave him, and through their friendship he found a way that led him into a deep intimacy with the essential spirit of their people and made it possible for him to help them as no other foreigner could. With Tagore as with Gandhi the acknowledgement of what Andrews did for him personally, as well as for his people, is grateful and sincere. In his preface to Andrews's posthumously published little book *The Sermon on the Mount*, he pays noble tribute to what he owed to his friend whose love, he says, "I believe to have been the highest blessing of my life." "Such a rare companionship of soul was a gift of God beyond all price. No lesser explanation on the human plane will suffice to account for it. In it there was no taint of selfishness, no stain of ambition, only a simple-minded offering of the spirit to its Lord. The question in the Kena Upanishad came into my mind unbidden: 'By whose grace was this soul sent to me, in what secret is rooted its life?' "

And what Andrews was to this great representative of India he was towards the whole of the people of the land. "He did not," Tagore goes on, "pay his respects to India from a distance with detached and calculated prudence. He threw in his lot without reserve in gracious courtesy with the ordinary folk of this land." In the realization and acceptance of all that this involved for him, an Englishman, he showed, Tagore goes on, "the moral strength and purity of his love. . . . He came to live with us in our joys and sorrows, our triumphs and misfortunes, identifying himself with a defeated and humiliated people." Andrews tells us in another of his books how that epiphet of "a defeated people" hurt the sensitive nature of the poet when, on the occasion of a visit of Tagore to Japan, the Japanese newspapers warned their country against this "prophet of a defeated nation." They had discovered that his mind was not racial and national like theirs, and that he hated war.

There were many others who were similarly bruised and humiliated among the people of India and to them the sympathy and understanding that Andrews's sensitive spirit was always able to supply brought consolation and strength for which they were deeply grateful. There may not have been many in India who were quite as sensitive as Tagore, but one such writes in his autobiography of what Andrews did for him. Jawaharlal Nehru does not seem to have been among his most intimate friends, but he tells us how moved he was by Andrews's "imaginative insight into the mind and heart of a hurt and helpless people." In a pamphlet that Andrews had published in 1920, called *Independence—the Immediate Need*, Nehru found, he tells us, "the feeling of the humiliation of India, a fierce desire to be rid of it and to put an end to our continuous degradation." "It was wonderful that C. F. Andrews, a foreigner and one that belonged to the dominant race in India, should echo that cry of our inmost being."

"Andrews," Nehru goes on, "had written that the only way of self-recovery was through some vital upheaval from within. The explosive force needed for such an upheaval must be generated within the soul of India itself. . . . It was with the intense joy of mental and spiritual deliverance from an intolerable burden that I watched the actual outbreak of such an inner explosive force as that which actually occurred when Mahatma Gandhi spoke to the heart of India the *mantram*[1] 'Be free! Be slaves no more!' and the heart of India responded."

The succour and strength that Andrews brought to the Indian people by his identification of himself with their cause is manifest in such testimonies as these in which Tagore and Nehru tell with deep feeling of what Andrews's life with and for them achieved. It was something imponderable that he bestowed on India but it was none the less rare and precious on that account, and it was given quite simply, as Tagore declares, by means of "his rare gift of spontaneous, universal friendship."

[1] That is, we may say, "the word of power."

3

Brother of the Poor

We have seen already from many instances how much the sorrows of India, and—more than anything else because it lay at the root of so many of these sorrows—its poverty, lay heavy upon Andrews's heart, as it did upon the hearts of his two friends, Gandhi and Tagore. Because so many in India saw that that was so, it came about that everywhere he became known as *Dinbandhu.* The title means "Brother of the Poor" or "of the Humble." In either sense the name could fitly be applied, but it is true that for him as for Mahatma Gandhi the poverty of India in the simple sense of the physical hunger of so many multitudes of its people is a basal fact in the appeal that India makes to them. Andrews was *Dinbandhu* in the literal sense of his willingness as a brother to share in the poverty of India's poor. So it also was with Gandhi. Whatever we may think of the economic value of his emphasis on the *charka* or hand spinning-wheel and upon hand-spun and hand-woven cloth, we cannot deny that in making them the symbols of his crusade he is placing at its centre what is India's central problem, the relief of the poverty of her peasantry. Andrews in an editorial in *Young India* makes this statement: "If the question is asked, What is the sum and substance of the charge which Mahatma Gandhi laid against the British government in India? it may be summed up in a single phrase. He charged them with the oppression of the poor." If that is considered too severe a charge to bring against a government that has done so much for India we may accept instead the much more moderate statement of the Viceroy, Lord Wavell, in his first address to the central legislature at Delhi: "We must lift the poor man of India," he said, "from poverty to security, from ill health to vigour, from ignorance to understanding, and our rate of progress must no longer be at the bullock-cart standard, but at least at the pace of the handy and serviceable jeep." Does not this imply a judgement upon past neglect?

But this Brother of the Poor was not content to limit his responsibility to bringing charges against the government of neglect of its duty of taking measures to relieve the physical poverty of India. He interpreted the word and his duty in a wider sense. Wherever he found Indians—for Indians had a special claim upon his sense of brotherhood—in any condition of distress that he could do anything to relieve, he placed himself at their disposal. We have seen how the first challenge of this kind that came to him was that which confronted him when he went to South Africa to stand by Gandhi in his championship of the indentured Indians there. "When Gandhi began his struggle in South Africa," Andrews tells us, "he found the name of India so sunk in public estimation that he himself and all his companions were commonly called 'coolies' even by men of education like General Botha. Within twenty-three years he raised the name of India to such a moral height that he left South Africa amid the generous farewells of Europeans who expressed their deep respect for him and his compatriots" (*Mahatma Gandhi's Ideas*, p. 293). A similar vindication of the rights and the reputation of other Indians overseas was now to be one of Andrews's first duties and one which was to occupy much of his time and strength during the rest of his life.

What the evil of indenture was may best be summed up in the measured words in which G. K. Gokhale described it in a speech to the Imperial Legislative Council of India denouncing the system:[1]

[1] These passages in Gokhale's speech are taken from Hoyland's *C. F. Andrews.*

"Under this system those who are recruited bind themselves, first, to go to a distant and unknown land, the the language and usages of which they do not know and where they have no friends or relatives. Secondly, they bind themselves to work there for any employer to whom they may be allotted, whom they do not know and who does not know them, and in whose choice they have no voice. Thirdly, they bind themselves to live there on the estate of the employer, they must not go anywhere without a written permit, and must do whatever tasks are assigned to them, no matter how irksome these tasks may be. Fourthly, the binding is for a certain fixed period, usually five years, during which time they cannot voluntarily withdraw from their contract and have no method of escaping from its hardships, however intolerable. Fifthly, they bind themselves to work during the period for a fixed wage which invariably is lower, and in some cases very much lower, than the wage paid to free labour around them. And sixthly and lastly, and this is to my mind the worst feature of the system, they are placed under a special law never explained to them before they left the country, and which is in a language which they do not understand, and which imposes on them a criminal liability for the most trivial breaches of the contract, in place of the civil liability which usually attaches to such breaches. Thus they are liable under the law to imprisonment with hard labour, which may extend to two or sometimes to three months, not only for fraud, not only for deception but for negligence, for carelessness, and . . . for even an impertinent word or gesture to the manager or his overseers. . . ."

Mr Gokhale goes on to describe how those simple and illiterate people are recruited by "the unscrupulous representations of professional recruiters who are paid so much per head for the labour they supply." He goes on to show in detail the iniquity of the system, the suffering it caused, which is made evident by the numerous suicides of workers, and the degradation it imposed on those subjected to it. He declared that it condemned the indentured labourers to "a life which, if not one of actual slavery was at any rate not far removed from it." He demanded that the government should bring the whole indenture system to an end so far as India was concerned.

That was the conflict in the cause of India in which Gandhi found himself involved in South Africa and it was in the course of that conflict that he discovered and used that weapon of Satyagraha which he was to wield so often in later years in a wider field. There Andrews discovered for himself in association with Gandhi, a mission from which he could not turn aside and a method of fulfilling that mission which he received as "a new religious truth which yet was not new but as old as the everlasting hills." He found in South Africa a way of helping India that led him out in many directions and laid upon him many burdens but that he could rejoice in, for he was throwing in his lot with the down-trodden and despised.

Gandhi was successful in his struggle in behalf of his country and his people and an agreement was arrived at with South Africa in 1914 which vindicated the reputation of Indians from the contempt which the name of "coolie" and the treatment of them as coolies had brought upon them. General Smuts, who came to this agreement with him, recognized Gandhi then and always since then as "a great man, one of the great men of the world, dominated by high spiritual ideals."

This was not, however, the end of the troubles of Indians in South Africa. In his book *What I Owe to Christ* Andrews speaks, apparently in 1932, of his being engaged in writing that book on a ship which was bringing him to South Africa for the seventh time and he adds that East and Central Africa had become almost as well-known to him as South Africa was. Nor was that his final visit. It was indeed inevitable that he should encounter in Africa challenges that he could not ignore that affected not Indians alone. Africa was the headquarters for the whole world of that race-hatred which Andrews saw threatening to poison the springs of humanity in all the relationships of men. While he defended Indians against its cruelties he found it necessary sometimes to defend Africans against Indians as well. He had to guard against any partisanship in his championship of Indians. Tagore tells how when the Indians in South Africa tried to keep the Kaffirs at a distance and treat them with contempt Andrews could not tolerate this and, in consequence, "the Indians of South Africa once imagined him to be their enemy" (*The Sermon on the Mount*, p. x).

Nevertheless the first claim upon him was that of oppressed Indians wherever they might be, and soon he was on his way on a similar errand to Fiji. Two things in regard to the Indians who had gone under indenture to that colony which he felt demanded investigation without delay were what he calls "the appalling statistics of suicides" among them and the fact that the same moral evils existed there as in Natal but that in Fiji they had gone far deeper. This latter condition was due to the sex-disproportion among them, since not more than forty women were recruited for indenture for every hundred men so recruited.

His first visit was paid in 1915 and a second followed in 1917. The report that he and W. W. Pearson, who accompanied him, submitted after the first visit strongly condemned the indenture system "as leading inevitably to moral degradation." On his second visit he found, he tells us, that the state of things was much worse than before; and an agitation was set on foot in India which aroused strong feeling throughout the country and so impressed the government of India that it accepted the popular will and brought recruiting to an end. On January 1, 1920, this whole system of recruiting Indian labour was finally abolished. A third visit was paid by Andrews to Fiji in 1936, when he was able to judge of the progress made by the Indians who had remained there during the sixteen years that had elapsed since they had been set free from the semi-slavery of indenture. He found that things had gone steadily forward. "In spite of indebtedness," he writes, "in spite of insecurity of tenure, in spite of a thousand other evils, the advance made . . . has meant a triumph of character whose value is very hard to over-estimate; for the change . . . has not only given good economic results; it has also provided a new social structure" (*India and the Pacific*, p. 37). "On all my journeyings among Indians abroad I have never seen such a complete transformation. It reveals a remarkable power of initiative." Even the old religion, he finds, has recovered its vitality, under the guidance of the reforming Arya Samaj and the "family life is being built up again on its old religious foundation."

Perhaps his estimate may be suspected of reflecting his own natural optimisim, but he was aware that there remained serious problems to be solved. Are the races to be unified or are the racial boundaries to be kept sacrosanct? How long must the franchise remain as heavily weighted on the side of the European as it now is? He classes the governments of Kenya and Fiji as both forming anomalies in British constitutionalism, with racial supremacy established and the colonial civil service kept racially exclusive as well. These and other problems presented by Indian settlements overseas similar to those found in Fiji are bound up with the major problem of India's own future within or outside of the British Commonwealth of Nations. What Andrews was doing there had its own significance for the solution of that immense problem.

Andrews was fully aware of this, and ends his book, *India and the Pacific*, on this note (p. 214): "The struggle for freedom and independence in India cannot be separated for a moment from the struggle that is always going on in the most distant colony where Indians are domiciled. A victory there is a victory for India itself. A defeat on the other hand, brings with it the deepest sense of humiliation." His hope in regard to this colony, as in regard to every one of the others with whose welfare he identified himself so fully, was that "the freedom that every Englishman has inherited as a birthright" would be handed on to them.

§

If that can be said of a distant outpost such as Fiji, and if the future of the Indians there has importance for India itself and India's future in relation to Great Britain, how much more shall we find this to be the case when we turn to Kenya, which is just at India's door. The aim of the English settlers there was, as one of them frankly described it, that "since South Africa has closed the back door into Africa, so that no Indian may enter Durban, in the same manner the British in East Africa must close the front door at Mombasa." They have been successful in establishing a complete colour-bar for the highlands of Kenya, reserving them exclusively for Europeans, but they sought to go further and turn the whole of Kenya into a "white oligarchy."

It was in connection with this struggle that Andrews came to know Kenya so well, for in 1923 intense feeling was aroused in India by a resolution adopted by the Kenya Europeans threatening an armed revolt if the names of the Indian settlers were placed on the voters' roll. In the hope of finding a solution of this dangerous situation a delegation of Indians, headed by the distinguished Liberal, Mr Srinivasa Sastri, went to London in 1923. Their request for a general electoral roll in Kenya for all persons capable of passing a minimum test of civilization might have been accepted as a just demand by the Colonial Office but in the end white prejudice once more prevailed. The question that then arose is one that is of crucial importance for the future of the British Commonwealth of Nations. Is it to be a commonwealth of free and equal peoples? Or are there to be those within it who on account of their colour are relegated to the position of "second-class citizens" and so to be subjected to the dominance of the members of the white races? It was in connection with this ominous decision in Kenya that Mr Sastri used the words that are often quoted by Andrews, "If Kenya is lost all is lost." This was, it seemed to him, the "acid test of the British Empire" and it remains so now when the question still hangs in the balance whether or not a free India will enter the British Commonwealth.[1]

At the same time it is right to remind ourselves that an agreement was reached in 1927 between the Union of South Africa and India as to the position of Indians in South Africa. This is the Cape Town Pact, by which "assisted emigration" was to be stimulated by a high bonus but to remain entirely voluntary, that in the case of Africa-born Indians who insisted on making South Africa their own country the Union government pledged itself to assist them in every way to attain the white standard of life in the Union. The significance of this compromise agreement—unsatisfactory as it is—is all the greater when we remember that it was negotiated on the one side by General Hertzog, "an extreme Boer nationalist," and on the other by Mr Srinivasa Sastri, an Indian of great distinction and high culture. Mr Sastri, we are told, captivated the Hertzog cabinet and a sequel to this achievement of his statesmanship was that he returned to South Africa, at the request of the Viceroy, Lord Irwin, and of Mahatma Gandhi, as the first "Agent" of the

[1] H. C. E. Zacharias, *Renascent India*, pp. 226 *ff*.

Indian government in that country. The "coolie" nation had to this extent at least been vindicated. It was not long, however, before it became evident that trouble was brewing again in South Africa, and Andrews in the last months of his life felt grave anxiety as to the future of Indians there.

There remains at the same time the danger, not yet by any means averted, that in British East Africa the principle of racial equality will be openly abandoned as it has been in South Africa. In Andrews's opinion the racial segregation of the Kenya highlands for European occupation, outside the townships, is "the worst blow that has been dealt against equal racial treatment for the colonies for a whole century."

His visits to colonies where "ex-indenture" Indians were to be found reveal his readiness to put himself to any inconvenience in their cause and demonstrate how fully he earned the title "Brother of the Poor." British Guiana, Trinidad, Jamaica, Mauritius, were among these. He tells us that half the population of Trinidad and British Guiana came originally from India. The question arises in regard to such groups whether they should continue to look to India as their home and turn to it in any time of distress for help, or should rather make a wholly new life for themselves where they have cast their lot. Thus in his report on his visit to British Guiana, Andrews tells how he found the Indians there suffering from a period of economic depression, with the result that their thoughts turned back to India and they desired to return there. Andrews had to tell them that Indian living conditions were on the whole even worse than those they were passing through and that at Calcutta he had found "a mass of stranded repatriates who were only too anxious to come back again to Demerara." In spite of this warning, he says, "the cry went on that it was better to die in India than to die in Demerara."

Andrews's account of his visit to British Guiana reveals how much hardship has to be undergone from time to time by colonies like this which suffer from periodical vicissitudes in their fortunes, and how much need there is that, as is now being realized in some measure in Great Britain, much more must be done than has been done in the past to assist those who have settled in these lands to achieve and to maintain a more satisfying life. Andrews also gives a grave warning of the consequences in such a colony as British Guiana of injustice that has been done to Indians elsewhere. "It is absolutely true to say . . . that Kenya and Natal have 'fouled the pitch' for Demerara." He concludes his report with the words, "When people leave their mother country to come abroad and make great sacrifices of habit and tradition in order to do so, it should at least be accepted as an axiom that the material conditions to which they come by immigration are superior to those they left behind in their mother country."

§

But it was not only Indians overseas whose conditions outraged Andrews's sense of justice and touched his compassionate heart. They were often, indeed, as in the case of the settlers in British Guiana, better off materially than their fellow countrymen in India. It was the political injustice inflicted upon a people who were looked down upon as uncivilized and degraded, rather than their poverty in the literal sense of the word, that moved him to champion their cause. He never forgot that in taking the side of Indians unjustly deprived of their rights as well as of their good name he was at the same time vindicating the liberal traditions of his own land and maintaining its honour. In the case of "the poor" within India's own borders the case is in some respects different. They too, in common with all the Indian people whether they are at home or abroad, have certain rights that they demand and certain wrongs that have been inflicted upon them, but in their case the source from which their poverty comes is more complicated than with those who have gone to seek their fortunes overseas. We have accordingly to look more closely at their woes and the causes of them.

That India suffers tragically from economic poverty is a fact beyond argument. That "India—along with China which is almost on the same level—is by all reckoning the poorest country in the world" and that its poverty "to-day seems to be increasing," Andrews affirms without any qualification: but we cannot accept a generalization as a fact when we have not sufficient data either to affirm or to deny. It remains unquestionably true, nevertheless, that India's poverty is extreme, that it is the basal fact of the human problem of its people, and that far more than has been done could be done and should be done to remedy it. That statement applies not only to the evils that come directly from undernourishment but also to those that are caused by diseases due to undernourishment or aggravated by it. These sorrows of the land may be said to be in part inflicted by man and in part by nature. Such a famine as that which has caused so much death and destruction in Bengal recently was due, as we can say without hesitation, to both of these causes unhappily coming together at a tragic moment in India's history. There are other catastrophes, such as earthquake and floods, that come with no human cause at work that we can discern, while others again are the results entirely of human cruelty and crime. All of these causes of suffering operate in India and of them all Andrews was well aware, and of the suffering that they brought upon the innocent as well as upon the guilty.

In the case of some of the worst of the evils that afflict India Andrews did not feel called to deal as directly or to assign blame for them as outspokenly as he did in the case of others. These were the evils that India's own people have inflicted, evils springing from old and warped traditions or religious beliefs that are wrong or have been perverted. Some evils,

E

for example, spring from the very Ahimsa—the "non-injury"—that, as interpreted by Gandhi, Andrews saw to be so noble. But when Gandhi, untrue to this partial truth when a higher truth guided him, put an end painlessly to the misery of a poor calf, a leader of Hindu orthodoxy threatened to shoot him. Andrews recognizes that an example emerges here of a problem that needs a higher wisdom than Hindu orthodoxy for its solution, and so he touches only lightly upon it. Gandhi had a full right to go further in vindicating a true Ahimsa than anyone not born a Hindu could, but he feels himself helpless before the spectacle of the holocausts of sheep and lambs slain for sacrifice at Kalighat in Calcutta. "I must go through more self-purification and sacrifice," he writes, "before I can hope to save these lambs from that unholy sacrifice. It is my constant prayer that there may be born on earth some great spirit, man or woman, who will deliver us from this heinous sin" (Gandhi, *My Experiments with Truth*, Vol. I, p. 548).

The case is similar with the evils that spring from the ancient and intolerable wrong of "untouchability." These evils must be condemned—as Andrews condemns them—and must be cured, but on the whole he himself leaves such evils alone in the belief that an India now awakened, or awakening, will itself carry through their cure. He recognizes how Christian missions in the past "rescued many thousands of these depressed classes from a life-long degradation that had sunk almost below the human level." "But," he goes on, "things have now entirely changed. Hinduism with inner faith and hope and courage is reforming itself. . . . The whole outlook has changed radically from what it was a century or even sixty years ago" (*The True India*, p. 148).

This tremendous problem, with the consequences that any real solution of it would bring to the unhappy people involved as well as to the reputation of India in the eyes of the world, probably weighed more heavily on his heart than any other of the woes of India. That this was so, and that he was aware that he could not take any effective part in bringing about that solution, is evident from a remarkable letter that he wrote to Gandhi in May, 1933. Gandhi was in prison at the time and had announced a twenty-one days' fast which was to be "a heart prayer for purification of myself and my associates for greater vigilance and watchfulness in connection with the Harijan ['untouchable'] cause." With this fast and its object Andrews was in entire sympathy and he wrote to Gandhi from England this very significant letter to say so. Then he goes on:

> "Haven't you been trying to serve two masters and if you have given your life as a hostage for 'untouchability removal' does not that mean entire concentration on that issue for the whole remainder of your life without turning to the right or to the left?
>
> "I want to work that out and 'think aloud' as you rightly put it. You staked your life itself on this one issue—removal of this curse. Can you now go and use that life in other secondary issues? I want you to answer that question. I am quite unworthy even to put it, because I haven't risked my life at all and am living here in comparative ease. . . .
>
> "You may say—and it may be right—that without Purna Swaraj [complete independence] you will always be blocked on this very question by some obstruction from an alien government. I can understand that argument. . . . But there is another moral argument that you have used again and again. It is this: 'We are not fit to attain Purna Swaraj while we go on treating our Harijan brothers and sisters like this.' You have all the moral force behind you if you are led to take this course—to say to the world, 'My life is now entirely a hostage for the Harijans'."

Gandhi's reply need not be given with any fullness; we are not concerned with him except in relation to Andrews, whose plea he puts aside on the ground that his life "is an indivisible whole." "I can't devote myself entirely to untouchability and say, 'Neglect Hindu-Muslim unity or Swaraj.' All these things run into one another and are interdependent." But it seems plain that Andrews was afraid that, as another great Indian, Swami Vivekananda, once confessed of himself, "I have become entangled," so it was with Gandhi. Politics had drawn him aside from what should have wholly absorbed him. Andrews, so far as we know, acquiesced in Gandhi's decision and put aside his doubts; but it is significant that he had doubts. His opinion quoted above that the whole outlook on untouchability had changed was certainly too optimistic. Immense difficulties had to be overcome and no one was equipped as Gandhi was to overcome them.

The entire removal of this blot from Indian life in the course of the present generation—which, he says, is the aim of educated India—would indeed be a miracle, as he recognizes; but, he adds, it is not impossible. Gandhi's example in this matter is visible to all India and it may work that miracle. Certainly every Christian who seeks the good of India will desire that this end may come and come speedily, and every Christian ought, as Andrews urges, "to welcome this advance from within Hinduism as a true movement of the Spirit of the living God" (*op. cit.*, p. 148). But Andrews's hopes for an advance from within Hinduism need not have prohibited him, or anyone who shares his desire for India's welfare, from helping up from the depths these submerged and outraged millions, in the name and by the power of Christ.

Concerning another indigenous evil, child marriage and the tragic consequences that follow, Andrews also makes his position quite clear. He stands side by side with India, seeking to divest himself of his foreignness and yet aware at the same time that he cannot wholly do so. Just because he is a foreigner, when he deals with evils that the people of India have themselves created, he cannot speak to them as frankly as Gandhi, for example, does. He tries to see, and does see, the explanations and extenuations that we ought to take into account when we blame them. We must remember, for example, that one cause of a high mortality in maternity cases is "the grinding poverty of the poor."

"I can well understand," he says, dealing with this subject, "that I am risking the inference being left by my words, that I am making light of acute human suffering of a very unbearable kind and taking the sting out of the stern warnings which nature gives, so that they fail to have their full effect of goading the public conscience of India into concerted action. . . . But to goad the public conscience effectively is like an act of surgery. And surgery needs a very skilful hand. . . . Nothing in the world does more harm than to wound sensitive public feeling by harsh incisions made in wrong places" (*op. cit.*, p. 125).

We must, we recognize, tread gently when we approach such ancient wrongs, and realize our own unrepented sins. Andrews has a chapter in *Mahatma Gandhi's Ideas* on "untouchability" to which he gives the title "Our Shame and Theirs." The phrase is Gandhi's and has reference to his sense of India's humiliation in the presence of that evil. Andrews in this chapter deliberately sets side by side as similar, and as being India's shame on the one hand and our shame on the other, "the caste feeling in India and the race prejudice in South Africa." We shall deal later with the shame that Andrews felt when he realized in South Africa that this race-prejudice had even become embedded in the Church at its very centre.

§

Something must now be said of how Andrews sought to help those suffering from such calamities as earthquakes and floods, and from the consequences that come from men's hostility and suspicion as we find them at work among the hill-tribes of the North-West Frontier of India. These will have to suffice as illustrating how he responded to many other demands upon his sympathy and help.

Earthquakes and floods are not infrequent in India but the earthquake of which Andrews wrote a brief account was of exceptional severity and destructiveness. The number of deaths that it caused, actually accounted for and recorded, according to the official figures was over 10,000. A leading Indian who took a large part in the organization of relief considered that the number could hardly be less than 20,000. It took place in North Bihar in January, 1934. Andrews was in London at the time but he did all that he could to make the calamity and its gravity known and to secure funds for the relief of the extreme necessity of a peasantry always living on the verge of destitution. Miss Agatha Harrison, who visited the stricken area with Gandhi, reports a striking estimate of the severity of the situation as she saw it: "It was said that the poverty of the men and women was at zero; the earthquake had divided this by ten."

As Andrews was not able to arrive till late in the year he had no actual experience of the famine that followed, and his help was mostly given from a distance. Even when he arrived, to find that an abnormally heavy monsoon had caused further miseries, his own ill-health limited the personal help he was able to render. He bears witness, however, to the fact that the desperate human need for a time at least overcame the dissensions that at other times caused in this province so much strife and division. Gandhi, Miss Harrison reports in a letter to Andrews, "Never commiserated with them in their misery. He presented them with a challenge: 'What has this calamity taught you? This is no time for differences between Congress and Government, between Touchable and Untouchable'." And in some measure at least this unity was achieved.

Another seemingly intractable evil, due in this case to human factors and not to the forces of nature, has long confronted India, and of it and Andrews's attitude to it something must be said. This is what, in the title of a book published by him in 1937, he calls *The Challenge of the North-West Frontier*. He describes the solution that he proposes in that book as "a contribution to world peace." He felt, it is evident, the urgent pressure of this subject on his heart and conscience because of the new method of dealing with frontier raids that the government of India had recently adopted. This consisted in the bombing of frontier villages from the air. The sharp controversy that had been aroused in India in consequence of the adoption of this method, and the resentment that the allegation of the bombing of women and children created, had some effect on the government, causing it to consider how retaliatory methods of repression could be modified and remedial methods adopted instead. These criticisms came to a head when the subject was debated in the Legislative Assembly in 1935.

Events that have happened since then in the second world war, the hideous devastation that has been caused by the bombing of cities, increase the urgency of the whole problem here involved and justify more than ever the sombre anticipations of Andrews. He reminds us that the action of the British government at the Air Disarmament Conference in 1933 in demanding that "air-bombing for police purposes in certain outlying districts" should be exempted from abolition, had "blocked," as he alleges, the efforts of the conference in the cause of peace and deprived

Great Britain of the moral initiative that she had previously held in that cause. In the Spanish civil war, "the murderous horror of the incendiary bomb shocked the civilized world," and we know how all that has happened since has deepened this horror. Perhaps the civilized world is by this time benumbed, but no one can put a limit to the ruin that threatens the whole world if the methods that were made use of on the Indian frontier, with the utmost moderation and for the ends of justice and the prevention of greater evils, were to become—as they have become—the instruments of unrestrained violence and passion. If it be indeed true that, as H. M. Tomlinson, whom Andrews quotes, affirms, we threw away the opportunity of preventing such a menace as this has proved to be "because we required a few bombers for a private purpose among hills so remote that most of us do not know exactly where they are," then we may well deplore the limitations of human foresight.

Another aspect of the situation on the Indian frontier that influenced Andrews greatly in setting forth his plan in 1937 was his confidence in the pacific disposition of the chief frontier leader at that time, Khan Abdul Ghaffar Khan, and the influence that he believed that Gandhi and his principle of Ahimsa had upon him. "Of one thing," Andrews writes, "I can speak with certainty at first hand, namely about the character of Khan Abdul Ghaffar Khan himself." "To find a Pathan leader," he says again, "practising Ahimsa or Non-Violence, enjoining it upon his followers and implicitly taking instructions from Mahatma Gandhi, reads almost like a legend or romance, but in reality it is a solid fact in modern Indian history." The "Frontier Gandhi" as this remarkable man has been called, declares in the strongest terms his devotion to non-violence. "I want the Pathan," he says, "to do to others as he would like to be done by. It may be I may fail and a wave of violence may sweep over my province. I shall then be content to take the verdict of fate against me" (*The Challenge of the North-West Frontier*, pp. 80, 84).

One cannot help suspecting that Andrews here, as in other instances that we have noted, may be too sanguine in his estimate of the possibility of so speedy a change, that mankind "of ancient crooked will" cannot be transformed all at once by the presentation to them of an ideal, however lofty. He wants that the traditional line of thought which India has inherited and can still reproduce should have full freedom of development in public policy. Khan Abdul Ghaffar Khan himself—and indeed Andrews also—have doubts of the success of the introduction of a Hindu principle among people so different from the Hindus as the Pathans of the frontier are. We are told that even the adherence of the North-West Frontier province to the Congress policy for India shows signs in the last year or two of weakening. Abdul Ghaffar is no longer a leading member of the Congress and his brother, who has succeeded him on the Congress working committee, has probably less influence over his fellow Muslims. Congress control of the Frontier Province seems now to be definitely interrupted.

Thus it is possible that Andrews's confidence in the possibility of applying Ahimsa to this province by the action of the Muslim people would not be confirmed by events. That does not, however, affect the validity of the policy that he presses upon the government of India. He links up his plan with his claim that India should be free to govern herself, and the question as to how in these circumstances the frontier is to be controlled would be a question for the independent Indian government to decide for itself, and such a government may not feel that the method of Ahimsa is applicable there. Andrews himself admits that there may be something to be said for approving even the policy of "police bombing" in very exceptional circumstances when peaceable methods had been tried and police work was found to be necessary.

Apart from this, however, the general policy of bringing such an area under humane and enlightened administration and endeavouring to win the goodwill of the inhabitants is what Andrews is here urging upon the attention of those, whoever they may be, British or Indian, who are responsible for the government of this area. Whether that policy is called by such a name as Ahimsa or by any other name, a measure of persuasion is surely better than one of brute force, and one that remedies abuses than one of retaliation. The present government of India has always recognized this, though it has pursued its aim at too slow a pace and with too little steadfastness of purpose. Andrews in advocating "a revised frontier policy" reminds us that this trouble is one that is not found on the Indian frontier alone, that it has yielded elsewhere to economic measures freeing people in similar circumstances from a life of poverty and enabling them to obtain a better living from their barren soil. He cites as a single example of the influence humane and skilled treatment can exercise upon such wild tribesmen the work that Dr. Pennell ("Pennell of the Frontier" as he was called) did among them by means of his hospital at Bannu. He quotes an English colonel, who knew the frontier well, as saying that "to have Dr. Pennell was worth a couple of regiments, so great a peace-maker he had become." He might also have quoted what Sir John Maffey, formerly governor of the Frontier Province, wrote of Mrs Starr, a nurse in a mission hospital in Peshawar. She went, at the governor's request, unarmed and unprotected, far into the mountains of Tirah: and because she was known for her work all through that turbulent region she was able to do so in perfect safety and to bring back an English girl who had been kidnapped. "By what she did," wrote Sir John, "she made a British mark upon the heart of Tirah that was better than the drums and tramplings of an army corps." It was more than a British mark; it was a Christian mark. A policy inspired by such a spirit as these instances exemplify is the true alternative—whether it be called by the Indian name of Ahimsa or by any other name—to the policy of "police bombing" or of frontier expeditions.

4

Christ's Faithful Apostle

THERE still remains for examination an aspect of Andrews's life and work which is indicated by the title of "Christ's Faithful Apostle," a title given to him because it fitted his initials and at the same time was true to what he was. By whom the name was first given is not apparently known, but when it was suggested it was at once recognized, not less by non-Christians than by Christians, as entirely appropriate and was frequently cited as such both during his life and after his death. Non-Christians never doubted that this was the fundamental fact in regard to him, explaining all else. It accordingly provides us with an appropriate opportunity of attempting a general appraisal of the abiding value of his life and of measuring it by a standard which he himself would have chosen. From the first day when he set foot on Indian soil, as he himself tells us, a new life began for him, and from then onwards he was a friend of the land and a brother especially of its humble people. But central to all that he was and did, "making it fair and like a lily in bloom," was his Christian faith and his Christian apostolate.

That this is true of him there can be no doubt at all and whoever first gave him this designation described him in a relationship which he sought to have, above all else, as the controlling factor in his whole life and service. In *What I Owe to Christ*, which is certainly the most notable of all his writings and has been recognized as a religious classic, looking back on the time when his life in India was opening before him, he sums up his religious experience. "After thirty years of life spent in the East," he writes (p. 152 *ff.*), "certain great facts in my own religious thinking stand out in the foreground. By far the greatest of these is this—that Christ has become not less central but more central and universal; not less divine to me but more so, because more universally human. I can see him as the pattern of all that is best in Asia as well as in Europe."

At intervals throughout his life when occasion to do so arose he publicly declared anew the central spring of renewal that he had first discovered when he was nineteen years old. Thus in 1927 he wrote at the request of a Japanese newspaper a statement of the faith that had sustained him through the years from that early experience. "Since that time," he says, "during more than forty-three years of incessant struggle, journeying to and fro throughout the world I have never lost the assurance of Christ's living presence with me. . . . He is no imaginative dream but a living Presence." Twelve years later, when his last illness was drawing near, he wrote a little book, *The Sermon on the Mount*, which was published after his death. In it he tells once more of this secret that so long before had first become his possession and that he had so often tested in the strain of living. "Christ has been the living Christ to me ever since and all my deepest thoughts have sprung from him." There could hardly be a more consistent life than that which he lived from that first day to his last.

It is true that a breach occurred in his religious belief and practice which in some degree turned it aside from the course that it had been pursuing, and which to some seemed to mean the actual abandonment of Christianity. Andrews passed during several years through an inner conflict as to his duty to the Church of England, of which he was an ordained minister. The conflict began early in his Indian career. He was himself in those days a high-churchman, but when he realized how such views as that attitude implied "separated him from those he loved in Christ Jesus" and made the deepest Christian fellowship, as represented by the partaking together of the Holy Communion impossible, he felt he could not hold that position any longer. He became aware of other difficulties as well when his friend Sushil Rudra protested against the Thirty-Nine Articles of English churchmen being imposed upon Christians belonging to the Indian tradition. He learned of these differences of outlook through his close friendship with Rudra and by seeing them through his Indian eyes. Again, his new sensitivity to his environment and its claims was further aroused at a Christmas Day service which was overshadowed for him when he heard the children reciting in Urdu the grim clauses of the Athanasian Creed. He was learning the lesson that never ceased to guide him through his Indian life, that he must see and feel through the eyes and the hearts of the Indian people and not remain imprisoned in his Englishness. The sense of his "bondage"—as all this seemed to his friend Rudra—under what in these matters his Church required of him became more and more intolerable. He had not yet, however, reached the stage of active revolt.

That stage was reached later when in South Africa he came face to face with grave evils, especially that of "the colour bar" and of racial discrimination, which he found to be "poisoning the wells of the Christian faith in almost every land abroad, leading irresistibly to a divided Christendom." It was in South Africa, as we have seen, that this became fully realized by him when he saw how Gandhi and others among his Indian friends were refused admission to many of the Christian churches. And yet these "were better Christians than we." "I had to stand on their side and not with those who were keeping alive the spirit of racial and religious exclusion." He wrote in a religious quarterly of his Church protesting against the moral evil that "threatened the Christian brotherhood principle." "The race cleavage," he declared, "has become embedded in the Church at its very centre—in the Sacrament," but his protest hardly stirred an echo in return (*What I Owe to Christ*, pp. 257, 263).

Finally, on his return from South Africa to Santiniketan, "when I saw," he says, "the pure face of the poet looking into mine I knew at once . . . that a final decision had there and then to be made." It was really no hasty step but the conclusion of a long moral struggle that had now lasted for several years. He wrote to his bishop, "telling him simply why I could not any longer conduct the Sunday services at Burdwan." "Since then," he goes on, "I have not taken any ministerial duties under a bishop, feeling that the subscription that I once gave to the Articles and the Book of Common Prayer no longer holds good. But I have remained throughout a communicant of the Anglican communion wherever I have gone" (*op. cit.*, pp. 268–9).

That was written probably in 1932. To complete the story of his emancipation from what he felt to be the bondage of beliefs which he had accepted when he took orders in the Church of England but which he was now no longer able to accept, a passage from an article that appeared in the magazine *Young Men of India*, in May, 1940, must be quoted. The writer tells how a day or two before Andrews underwent the operation which was followed by his death he wrote a letter to a friend in order to remove misunderstanding as to his Christian position and his final attitude to his own Church. In this letter he explained that the matters—or at least some of them—that had raised a difficulty of conscience for him many years before no longer caused such a difficulty because of the revision of the Book of Common Prayer "as now used in India," and in consequence he had been able "to resume the full duties of the Christian ministry."

§

But whether it was as a priest of the Church of England or as a prophet of the living God that Andrews discharged his ministry no one can deny that he bore the marks, if ever any man did, of a Christian saint. St. Francis Xavier,[1] a forerunner of his in India, along with much that was in strong contrast with what Andrews felt himself called to be and do in India, was in some of his qualities of sainthood strikingly like his modern successor. "He went barefoot," it is said of St. Francis, "with a poor torn gown. Everyone loved him dearly." We have seen how like Andrews was to that picture. It could as well be said of him as was said of the earlier saint that he was "like a whirlwind of love." We sometimes feel as if no man could love so many with such a warmth of love as he was aware of within his heart. But there are some who, whether by nature or by grace, are furnished with a greater capacity for this divine quality than others, and among those he must take a high place. Continually in India, he tells us, "it is as if I saw Christ in the faces of those I met." We need not try to explain this quality of his saintliness otherwise than by his possession of that insight and the heart to respond to it. It was that quality which, as we have seen, made it possible for him to be so great a friend.

Another of the marks he possessed, identifying him as belonging to the great succession of the Christian saints, was the spirit of joy that accompanied him in all his toils. We have seen how "eager people" came to Andrews asking him for the secret of "his evident joy and gladness." This was a quality that he himself was aware of as welling up within him, and he could have testified with Tertullian that the Holy Spirit is a glad Spirit. He tells us in one place how when the long weariness and strain of watching by the sickbed of an Indian student in Germany ended at last, "after the hurricane had passed over me and the deep waters had wellnigh overwhelmed me, the dear presence of my Lord and Master came like sunshine into my life, filling it once more with

[1] *The Life of St. Francis Xavier*, by Edith Ann Stewart [Mrs Robertson].

gladness" (*Christ in the Silence*, p. 37). It could certainly be said of many young Indians, brooding and unhappy, that they found their way to him, as it is said that St. Francis Xavier's brother Jesuits did to him also, and were made happy again by looking on his face.

There is yet another characteristic of some Christian saints that he possessed and that he shared with this earlier apostle to India. It is said that once Francis was heard in his sleep to cry out "More, more, more," and it was found that in his dreams he had been asking that he might suffer more and yet more for Christ. So it seems to have been with Andrews. He cannot be described as an ascetic, and in this respect he found himself opposed to Gandhi, especially to Gandhi's emphasis upon celibacy. "The human body," he writes, "to Gandhi is an evil not a good." He notes the difference between him and Tagore in this respect, Tagore affirming in a well-known poem, "Deliverance is not for me in renunciation," while Gandhi is possessed by the negative aspect of sin, "which has to be rooted out by an almost violent self-discipline." The contrast in this respect between the two men is striking and we have seen already how it often caused estrangement. In this matter Andrews was in agreement with Tagore rather than Gandhi. It was not austerity but love that guided him as it guided St. Francis. A sentence from the Sermon on the Mount that meant much to him was the question, τί περισσὸν ποιεῖτε; (Matt. v. 47), which he translates, "What do ye to excess?" Have you given, that is, as he explained it, to the extreme limit of love? He had these words in the Greek original on his study table when he was a student in Cambridge and fifty years later he was asking himself the same question in the last book he wrote. He saw in this "the tremendous test which Christ puts on our allegiance when he tells us, 'For my sake go even to this excess of love, and be prepared even to love your enemies'." He saw then with clear vision the loftiness of

Christianity, how it possessed, as he says in this final utterance of his mind, "a distinctive and precious quality which has made it unique among all the religions of the world." That was the level at which (and he testifies that it was so in his own experience "at periods, however brief") "every exercise and sacrifice of the will appeared to be joyfully possible" (*The Sermon on the Mount*, pp. 135, 136, 137).

These are some of the qualities of Andrews's religion that reveal the sources of energy that lay behind a life so strenuous and so selfless—a life also that drew men to him by its ardour and its attractive power. One other aspect of his religious life, that was written across it all from first to last and that proclaimed past all doubting its sincerity, was the way in which for him belief and action were inseparably bound together. In the preface to *What I Owe to Christ* he states this with an emphasis of strong conviction. "Christ ... seeks from us deeds not words: Devotion to him is in the first place not sentimental but practical. ... If [the Christian faith] has no power to restore or recreate the human will leading on to deeds of unselfish service, then it stands self-condemned" (p. 15). Such a passage as this—and all that so fully confirms it in his life—is a sufficient answer to the charge of sentimentalism so often brought against Andrews. Such "theopathic saintliness," as William James describes it,[1] was not his. We have here indeed a feature of the witness that Andrews's life bore to his Christian belief which reached very deep in its significance and spoke to India—indeed, we may say, to the world—with something like apostolic power. It is this element in his influence which might well be called revolutionary, for the need for it is urgent in those who profess the Christian religion and preach it.. It was indeed this which once turned the world upside down and which may do so again to-day if Andrews's example is followed.

[1] *Varieties of Religious Experience*, p. 345.

The unmistakable reality of Andrew's religion and this power that it possessed "to build above the deep intent The deed, the deed" commended it to those who watched him in India and wherever he went. Gandhi has frequently urged upon Christians, and especially upon Christian missionaries, to refrain from telling India about Christ and instead to live the Christian life; but Andrews, while agreeing with his opinion, did not confine himself too closely within its bounds. He certainly "told" the Christian message by his life in every province of India, and that message was never proclaimed more effectively than it was by him. His theory of leaving the Hindu to his own religion is difficult to reconcile with his affirmations, one of which has just been quoted, of the uniqueness of Christianity among the faiths of the world; and none of his friends, certainly not Gandhi himself, was unaware, when they called him, as they so often did, a true Christian, how high a place they were giving him. This "reality" that spoke so loud in his life, as well as the happiness that accompanied it, and that shone from him, drew to him young people everywhere. His own experience was that "radiance" shone upon him just in proportion as the test of seeking to do God's will in daily life was sincerely applied. So, as we have seen, young people came to him asking him for his secret of joy. He himself sought to appeal to "the energizing joy of youth as a gift gloriously meet for the Master's use." For that reason he was able to remain in close touch with "the young student world" all his life, for he had within himself the life of Him who, as an early Christian document expresses it, "is born at all times young in the hearts of the holy."

In "the young student world" whom he drew to himself and to whom he was drawn irresistibly there was no section that he desired more to serve and whose need of his glad spirit was greater than the students of India. They often asked him of the religious source of the radiance that they saw in him and coveted, and he, we can be quite sure, was never unwilling to tell them in plain words what that source was. He tells us how he found on his return to the West after long absence that "joy had entered into human life once more." He found it "in the Oxford Fellowship, in the World Student Federation, in the youth movements and the colleges of many lands." But there were many sections of youth among whom he must have found that this joy was something passionately desired but not yet attained. That was so at the time of which Andrews was speaking, namely about 1932, among the youth of Germany, and that was, and is so, also among the youth, especially the student youth of India. The causes which brought about this loss of what may be said to be a vital necessity for the young were largely the same in both lands. In 1931 there were in Germany, we are told, "about forty thousand unemployed university people" who, in consequence, could no more look into the future with anything like happiness or confidence. "The same situation had about the same time cast a deep shadow over the lives of the students in the universities of India. And behind that fear there lay in both cases still deeper causes for despair. The young intellectuals of both countries had for years been undergoing a process of disintegration and disillusionment. The past and the present had fallen apart and a chasm had opened between them. Thus they found themselves forlorn individuals in a nation into which they were unable fully to integrate themselves and in which they had little hope of building up such a fellowship as was essential to the fulfilment of their lives. With what that situation has developed into in Germany as a result of the appeals and promises of Hitler we have no concern here, but what young Germany needed and what the Leader who arose among them claimed to give them was what Indian students also needed and still need and in their souls desire. They need "a new conception of their value and of their place both in the cosmic order and in the world around them."[1]

In India not a few of the students who became acquainted with Andrews seem to have turned to him as representing what they felt so deeply that they lacked. His was a manifestly integrated life; fellowship was a precious reality to him and he gave it freely to them out of his abundance. He lived as one who possessed an assurance of "his place in the cosmic order," or—to express it in religious language—of his place in the divine purpose of love, as a member of the family of the divine Father. These religious convictions formed the living spring from which flowed the unfailing happiness and joy that they longed to possess as he possessed it.

Rabindranath Tagore's sensitivity of nature reveals what was felt by so many and he may be taken as representing their spirit—half resentment and half longing—at its finest. We have seen already how deeply hurt he was by the taunt cast at him in Japan of belonging to a defeated nation. The West drew him but he felt himself bound up with the East and sharing its sorrows and its humiliation. "This has been the reason," he said, addressing an audience in London, "why the West has not yet come home to our heart, why we struggle to repudiate her culture. It is because we ourselves are under the dark shadow of her dominance." The conflict, reflected in the clear mirror of Tagore's magnanimous nature, embittered many hearts among the young people of the land. And for them, as even for Tagore himself, Andrews became a symbol of an attainment that seemed, because of their lack of freedom and of the self-respect that accompanied freedom, to be beyond their reach. "There are screens between us," Tagore wrote to his friend, "which have to be removed—possibly they are due to the too great inequality of circumstances and opportunities between the

[1] E. Amy Buller, *Darkness over Germany*, p. 158; also p. 119.

two parties. . . . I cannot tell you how thankful I feel to you, who have made it easier for me to love your people. For your own relationship with India has not been based upon a sense of duty but upon genuine love. It makes me feel sad when I see this lesson of your life being lost—when it fails to inspire our people with the realization that love of humanity is with you far truer than patriotism" (*Letters to a Friend*, pp. 181 *ff.*).

He saw the lesson of Andrews's love being lost because its full depth was not realized. There were screens between them, barriers that the love of a single Englishman could not overcome. The young people he spoke to with such warmth of feeling could not hear all that he had to say because of the tumult of their patriotism in their own ears. As Tagore says in another of his sorrowful surveys of the situation, "The East was not ready to receive the West in all her majesty of soul. We have not seen what was great in the West because we have failed to bring out the great that was in ourselves."[1] Once at Oxford, Andrews tells us—once of many times, it is quite evident—an Indian student asked him what the source was of the spiritual power by which men could sacrifice themselves for others gladly. "I could only tell him," Andrews says, "from my own experience that it was the daily presence of the living Christ claiming them by His love that had wrought this love in return" (*What I Owe to Christ*, p. 305). What more was there to tell? But the chasm remained.

There we see "Christ's Faithful Apostle" seeking to do for the youth of India what has been done elsewhere so tragically amiss, showing to them from his own experience what could transform their dull tasks and could give their little existence a cosmic significance and an eternal destiny. Andrews saw clearly that the political situation in India at the present thwarts the efforts and blights the hopes of the

[1] Quoted in *India and Britain*, p. 37.

youth of the land, making their lives dull and insipid and meaningless. That was what made him take up their political cause with such fervour and conviction. On our part the debt of honour that we owed had to be paid and the shadow that darkened the sun for them had to be lifted. He championed the good elements in Hinduism and in Islam—sometimes, perhaps, too blindly—just because religion was bound up with so much that still brought comfort to their lives. But he saw beyond that partial good quite clearly their orphaned condition in a universe that had only a dim and shadowy deity shining bleakly and remote upon them. After telling of the question that the Indian student asked in Oxford and of his answer he goes on to affirm that "human life would sink back incredibly far, beyond all recovery whatsoever if it were not for the supreme miracle of grace that Christ's presence has brought to mankind" (*op. cit.*, p. 307).

§

This brings us to the duty of examining Andrews's conception of his apostolate or, to put it otherwise, his missionary vocation, and what it involved. Did he put it aside when he surrendered his priestly ministry under a bishop but retained his prophetic ministry as that for which he was "fitted and prepared by God"? We needed, he believed, to become "first-century Christians" once more (*op. cit.*, pp. 270, 209). What did that involve for him in India, as for Albert Schweitzer in Africa, whose example moved him so much? What he says on "proselytizing" and on the relationship to each other of the religions of the world opens up great questions on which Andrews's sincerity and devotion give him a right to speak and which have crucial importance for the Church of Christ. They cannot be dealt with fully here but they cannot be passed by.

For his knowledge of Hinduism Andrews was in the main

indebted, it is evident, to his friendship with Mahatma Gandhi and with Rabindranath Tagore. Neither of these could be counted an orthodox Hindu. Gandhi belongs by his family tradition to the *bhakti* or devotional Hinduism of the Vaishnavas, which is a theistic type of Hinduism that has a long history down the centuries. Tagore belonged to the modern eclectic theism of which his father and Raja Ram Mohan Roy were the first architects and which is indebted both to the *bhakti* tradition and to Christianity. It is not necessary to add anything to what has been already said of the lofty religious character of both these men nor to emphasize the fact that in each case the religion is a deeply realized, inward and ethical experience. It would be true also to say that each of them, while—in Gandhi's case certainly and probably also in Tagore's—claiming to be a Hindu, was a quite exceptional Hindu. Tagore could be more accurately described, as his Hibbert Lectures, *The Religion of Man*, make clear, as a humanist, though belonging to what Professor Irving Babbitt has described as "the least humanist of lands." The negations of Vedantic Hinduism were abhorrent to him much more than they were to Gandhi for whom, as we have seen, asceticism has a peculiar—and a peculiarly Hindu—attraction. Gandhi says of Tagore that he had "a horror of everything negative. His whole soul seems to rebel against the negative commandments of religion." That horror is really a consistent theist's horror of the barrenness of monistic Hinduism. It is to be found in Andrews as well as in Tagore, for with his conversion he escaped, he tells us, from "the impossibility of worshipping an unknown God who can only be described by negatives" (*op. cit.*, p. 101). But when Hindu negations are in question Tagore is more ready to express his "horror" than Andrews. Tagore indeed says frankly that monistic Hinduism "is not a religion" (*The Religion of Man*, p. 117).

When, therefore, Andrews speaks of Hinduism as he saw

it in the religion of his two friends he is not really speaking of what we may call central Hinduism. Even putting aside, as he, of course, deliberately does, and as they do also, all idolatry, the religion by which they lived and which he saw in them represents only a fraction of the highly diversified Hindu system. Nevertheless he often generalizes in regard to what he calls Hinduism when what he says is only relevant to a part of it. To take a single but important example—in *Mahatma Gandhi's Ideas* he has a passage which deals with the Hindu conception of God. "The word 'God'," he writes (p. 34), "without any further connotation, is well-known in every Indian language and is constantly on every Hindu's lips. The name of God is written on every Hindu's heart and when he thinks of God he thinks of him as One and Supreme. In all my intimate talks on religion with Mr Gandhi, amid many divergences and shades of contrast, I have never felt that there was any real difference between us with regard to this intimate belief. Here we were on common ground. In this sense Mr Gandhi is a theist and so am I; to both of us belief in God is as certain and immediate as our own personal existence."

What Andrews says here of Gandhi's conception and his own being closely akin is, no doubt, true, but when he takes for granted that the same can be truly said of the conception of God that is behind "the word that is constantly on every Hindu's lips," that is far indeed from being the case. Gandhi himself would not make any such claim. He admits frankly that while Hindu, Musalman and Christian all believe in God "we may each of us be putting our own interpretation on the word 'God'. . . . But what does that matter?" (*op. cit.*, p. 95). A Christian surely thinks—and Andrews certainly thought, as passages already quoted show—that it does matter.

That there is no doubt of this in the case of Andrews's own religious convictions is clearly shown if we turn to what he wrote three years later of the character of God as revealed in Christ compared with what the word "God" conveys in other religions. In *What I Owe to Christ* he writes (p. 218): "No one can know the Father as [Jesus] does or reveal him as Jesus can, because—that is his great secret—he and his Father are one. He is the Son of God, not in any narrow, abstract, metaphysical sense, which has no moral meaning, but in a deep, spiritual sense of oneness: one in mind, one in will, one in purpose, one in character itself. Herein, in the character of God, is the profoundest religious change that Jesus offers to all human estimates and values. It is a change so deep, so original, so incredibly simple, that it makes the Christian faith a new religion indeed—not a compendium merely of what had gone before but startling in its originality, and in its outward results nothing less than a fresh beginning in human history."

In the two passages quoted Andrews is speaking of the same thing—the character of God—as seen by Hinduism and by Christianity respectively. Can it be said that they are the same? "The narrow, abstract, metaphysical sense" of the word God, "which has no moral meaning" is the prevailing Hindu view which affects even the ordinary Hindu deeply and influences his whole life, and Andrews, of course, repudiates it, as Tagore would have repudiated it. Even Gandhi does so. Bal Gangadhar Tilak, the powerful popular figure who preceded Gandhi in the remarkable influence that he exercised all over India, was not a theist like Gandhi. He was an orthodox Hindu, a Vedantist, a man of great learning and high personal character. But Gandhi says of him: "He used to challenge my view of life and bluntly would say truth and untruth were only relative terms but at the bottom there was no such thing as truth or untruth, just as there was no such thing as life or death." Gandhi was, of course, poles apart from the purely metaphysical conception of God's nature which lies behind that view of life and which certainly has no moral meaning. There can be no harmony between a religious life which is built upon that foundation and the religious life that is built upon the revelation of God the Father that comes to us by Jesus Christ, His Son.

There is in Indian legend a famous story told by a Hindu poet of the sixteenth century called Tulsi Das, a story which Andrews more than once uses to illustrate his own religious outlook. The story tells how a seeker after God turned away from Brahman, "the unbegotten, the indivisible, the immaterial"—that is to say, the wholly negative—saying, "This lays no hold of my heart." "Tell me," he said, "how to worship the Incarnate," that is, the personal deity Rama. He desired worship, not speculation. There is, in contrast with this, another more modern Indian tale of a *sannyasi* or Hindu ascetic, a typical product of Vedantic orthodoxy, who when he was dying a violent death looked up at his murderer and said, "And thou, too, art He." That conception of the nature of God, with its resulting identification of God and man, is what some Hindus suppose Jesus meant when He said, "I and my Father are one." But neither Andrews nor any Christian would agree with them for a moment. A conception of the nature of God which, denying the difference of good and evil, places Him or it beyond them both is of course the very negation of the Christian faith. It has, however, a powerful position in the religious thought of India and has done much to mould Indian character.

Enough has been said to make it clear that Andrews's generalizations in regard to Hinduism have to be accepted with caution. It cannot be of this widespread and powerfully influential doctrine of monism, so destructive of moral effort, that he was thinking when he wrote, "The East represents the Eternal Divine Spirit . . . as unmanifest, yet he is mirrored by the pure in heart in the depth of the human heart." It is hard to find "the clue to the organic unity of the religious history of man in the East and West" which Andrews tells us he was seeking (*op. cit.*, pp. 156, 301), when we realize the flat contradiction between the Christian faith and this acosmic monism of which he was undoubtedly aware and which he from time to time specifically condemns. He had a favourite Shakespearian quotation which we can appropriate as applicable here. In the terrible words of Hamlet we have come "between the fell, incensed points Of mighty opposites."

What Andrews is really pressing upon our notice is not so much a theory of the unity of all religions as a warning against what Gandhi once called "doing a religious thing in an irreligious way." He is warning us against seeking to win a victory for Christianity by un-Christian and even anti-Christian methods. He is denouncing what Tagore bitterly described as being "like a coolie recruiter trying to bring coolies to his master's tea-garden." No doubt there are more reputable disguises that proselytizing often adopts and everyone who takes up the high vocation of being an apostle of Christ has to be on his guard against them all. A friendship made with a saintly Musalman, such as Munshi Zaka Ulla, if it was made with a view to winning him to the Christian faith, would have seemed to Andrews a deceit, an act of treachery to love. And yet we may be quite sure that, if his friends asked him—as many of his non-Christian friends did—to unveil to him the most precious of his spiritual possessions, he would have done so, and surely he would have rejoiced if his friend came to share with him in that Supreme Good "which is death to hide." The word "proselyte" applies to unworthy methods of presenting the Christian message and securing adherents to it, methods of pressure or enticement that are themselves denials of a true love and a true reverence for human personality. These methods he denounced and his recoil from them sometimes seems to carry him further than is necessary or even right.

But in such matters as these what is chiefly demanded is a tender and very sensitive conscience, true to the obedience that we render to the Lord of our lives and to His spirit which we proclaim and seek to represent. That, we are well assured, is the tribunal before which Andrews set his own conduct and tested his own motives.

There can be no doubt, of course, as he, and Gandhi also, were continually pointing out, that, in Andrews's words it is "infinitely more important to act out silently the Christian faith than to make professions about it"; but to proclaim the Christian message is a somewhat different matter and it is for that that the apostle is sent forth. That proclamation is indeed most effectively made through the fragrance of a truly Christian life, as Rudra held and as Andrews's own life demonstrates for all to recognize. Such silent influence is "worth all the propaganda teaching in the world." Nevertheless for Andrews, and for everyone who is entrusted with the good tidings of great joy which shall be for all people, silence cannot be, and was not even in his own case, the rule. Andrews, indeed, disliked, and refrained from, argument, and it has to be recognized that argument is often unprofitable in this kind of situation. This is especially so when, as with Andrews, the faith by which he lives and to which he testifies, is, as he says it was, "a spiritual consciousness, not an intellectual definition" (*op. cit.*, pp. 21, 165, 103). But witness has to be borne to the message and to the experience that accompanies it, and Andrews did not deny himself that privilege.

In all Andrews's warnings against "aggressiveness" in this matter one thing that is always restraining him is his sense of the nationalist spirit that was abroad in India and the inhibitions, as well as the sensitiveness to any suggestion of inferiority, that that spirit created in the minds of his Indian friends. At the same time these warnings were addressed to the foreigner, because Andrews saw as one of the most serious faults of at least the British foreigner his tendency to *impose* truth rather than to share it, to present his message, even when it was the message of the divine love, as if it was *his* gift rather than God's.

These reflections should cause us to consider anew the methods we should use so as to secure that the Christian message is conveyed to India and to every non-Christian land in a fully Christian way. But that concern must not preclude us, as Andrews, one feels, allowed it sometimes to preclude him, from recognizing and condemning evils that in India have issued, in part at least, from wrong thoughts of God and life and duty. Of that enough has been already said. It is indeed true that the reformation of gross abuses in India must be achieved by the children of that land themselves, and any denunciation of them by us must be restrained and must make full allowance for the failure of us all to live up to our professions. Just as we recognize that failure, and stand beside them, as Andrews did, encouraging them, they will feel the more free to denounce the evils in their society and to search out the roots in their own ancient doctrines from which these evils have sprung. Such doctrines as that of *Maya*, or the unreality of all life and duty, and that which declares—in a common popular saying—that "the doer and the Causer to do are one," with its resulting fatalism, are deadly breeding grounds for social wrongs and miseries. When one thinks of the sorrows of India one desires to see arising in that land not only those who demand her freedom but also many like those leaders in social reform whom India has had and still has, who, knowing what those evil roots are, will denounce them with even Voltairian violence and call upon their countrymen, as Voltaire did, "*écraser l'infame.*"

Andrews did not conceive that he was called to that duty, and in the circumstances of India at the present time it was probably not his duty. His duty, as he saw it, was to see that justice was done to India in her political and economic life and that liberty and self-respect were restored to her. He saw clearly that the sense of their wrongs and of their being, as Tagore bitterly described them, "a defeated and humiliated people" had created deep bitterness and resentment. He accordingly gave himself without reserve to the removal of these evils and he sought, to that end, to identify himself in every respect with them and with the new hopes and aspirations that were awaking within them. He gave them these things through the exceptional power of affection that he possessed and that was profoundly deepened and irradiated by the love of God that had come to possess him and govern him.

§

Looking back across the life he lived for nearly forty years in India's cause we realize afresh the consistency and unwavering courage of it and see their only explanation in the Source from which they issued and to which he always ascribed whatever in him was of worth. Rabindranath Tagore, because of his finely sensitive nature, was able perhaps better than any other of his friends to interpret his spirit. He saw how much Andrews gave up for India and how "out of his English tradition he brought to India his English manhood." His life had nothing in it of complaint for this exchange. He believed himself to have been richly rewarded and few indeed have won so rich a prize as was his in India's affection for him.

Andrews was no *deracine* Englishman. There was what someone in another connection has called "a passionate ambivalence" in his life as he toiled for India and looked back to England. Both lands were in his heart and he sought that both should remain united in friendship and in a deeper understanding than they had yet reached. This is one goal to which he looked that is not yet attained.

But surely Tagore was right when he said of him, "His love for Indians was a part of that love of all humanity which he accepted as the law of Christ." The name that fits him best of all is, as we have seen already, an Indian name, *Jagadmitra*, "Friend of All the World." So it is fitting that the final word in regard to him should be with his friend Rabindranath Tagore whom he called *gurudeva*, "revered teacher," and who shared with him his love of humanity. "This," he said, "is what I would say to you in solemn confidence at the moment when his lifeless body is being committed to the dust—his noblest gift to us, and not only to us but to all men, is a life which is transcendent over death itself, and dwells with us imperishably."